The Selected Works of Nikita Khrushchev
First Prism Key Press Edition 2011

Prism Key Press
New York, NY 10001
PrismKeyPress.com

ISBN-13: 978-1468101003

The Selected Works of Nikita Khrushchev

CONTENTS

Obituary of G.M. Dimitrov

Georgi Mikhailovitch Dimitrov was born on June 18, 1882, in the town of Radomir, of a proletarian revolutionary family. When he was only 15 years old, the young Dimitrov, working as a compositor in a printshop, joined the revolutionary movement and took an active part in the work of the oldest Bulgarian trade union of printers.

In 1902, Dimitrov joined the Bulgarian Workers' Social Democratic Party. He actively combated revisionism on the side of the revolutionary Marxist wing of Tesnyaki led by Dimitri Blagoyev.

The self-sacrificing revolutionary struggle of Dimitrov earned him the warm love of the revolutionary workers of Bulgaria, who, in 1905, elected him secretary of the Alliance of Revolutionary Trade Associations of Bulgaria. In that post he remained right up to 1923, when that alliance was disbanded by the fascists.

While leading the struggle of the Bulgarian proletariat, Dimitrov displayed courage and staunchness in the revolutionary struggles, was repeatedly arrested and persecuted. In the September armed uprising of 1923 in Bulgaria he headed the Central Revolutionary Committee, set an example of revolutionary fearlessness, unflinching staunchness and devotion to the cause of the working class. For his leadership of the armed uprising in 1923 the fascist court sentenced Dimitrov in his absence to death. In 1926, after the provocative trial, engineered by the fascists, against the leadership of the Communist Party, Dimitrov was again sentenced to death in his absence.

Compelled, in 1923, to emigrate from Bulgaria, Dimitrov led the life of a professional revolutionary. He worked actively in the Executive Committee of the Communist

International.

In 1933, he was arrested in Berlin for revolutionary activity. During the Leipzig Trial, Dimitrov became the standard-bearer of the struggle against fascism and imperialist war. His heroic conduct in the court, the words of wrath which he flung in the face of the fascists, exposing their infamous provocation in connection with the Reichstag fire, unmasked the fascist provocateurs and roused new millions of workers throughout the world to the struggle against fascism.

In 1935, Dimitrov was elected General Secretary of the Executive Committee of the Communist International. He waged a persistent struggle for the creation and consolidation of the united proletarian and popular front for the struggle against fascism, against the war which the fascist rulers of Germany, Japan and Italy were preparing. He called untiringly on the masses of the working people of all countries to rally around the Communist Parties in order to bar the way to the Fascist aggressors.

Dimitrov did great work in the ranks of the international Communist movement in forging the leading cadres of Communist Parties loyal to the great teachings of Marxism-Leninism, to the principles of proletarian internationalism, to the cause of the defense of the interests of the people's masses in their respective countries.

During the Second World War, Georgi Dimitrov called on the Communists to head the national-liberation anti-fascist movement, and tirelessly worked at organizing all patriotic forces for the rout of the fascist invaders. He led the struggle of the Bulgarian Workers' Party (Communists) and all Bulgarian patriots who rose in arms against the German-fascist invaders.

For his outstanding services in the struggle against fascism he was, in 1945, awarded the Order of Lenin by the Presidium of the Supreme Soviet of the U.S.S.R.

After the defeat of fascist Germany, Georgi

Mikhailovitch Dimitrov led the building of the new People's Democratic Republic of Bulgaria, and laid the foundation for the eternal friendship between the Bulgarian people and the peoples of the Soviet Union. Untiringly working for the consolidation of the united anti-imperialist camp and the rallying of all democratic forces, Georgi Mikhailovitch Dimitrov mercilessly exposed the betrayal of the cause of Socialism and the united anti-imperialist front by Tito's nationalist clique.

In the person of Dimitrov, the working people of the whole world have lost an ardent fighter, who gave all his heroic life to the supreme service of the cause of the working class, the cause of Communism. The death of Dimitrov is a great loss to the whole international working class and Communist movement, to all fighters for lasting peace and a people's democracy. By his self-sacrificing struggle in the ranks of the working-class movement, by his boundless devotion to the great teachings of Lenin and Stalin, Dimitrov earned the warm love of the working people of the whole world.

The life of Dimitrov, loyal comrade-in-arms of Lenin and Stalin, staunch revolutionary and anti-fascist champion, will serve as an inspiring example to all fighters for the cause of peace and democracy, for Communism.

Farewell, our dear friend and comrade-in-arms!

Andreyev, Beria, Bulganin, Voroshilov, Kaganovitch, Kosygin, Malenkov, Mikoyan, Molotov, Ponomarenko, Popov, Pospelov, Stalin, Suslov, Khrushchev, Shvernik, Shkiryatov.

Speech to 20th Congress of the C.P.S.U.

(Delivered February 1956)

Comrades! In the Party Central Committee's report at the 20th Congress and in a number of speeches by delegates to the Congress, as also formerly during Plenary CC/CPSU [Central Committee of the Communist Party of the Soviet Union] sessions, quite a lot has been said about the cult of the individual and about its harmful consequences.

After Stalin's death, the Central Committee began to implement a policy of explaining concisely and consistently that it is impermissible and foreign to the spirit of Marxism-Leninism to elevate one person, to transform him into a superman possessing supernatural characteristics, akin to those of a god. Such a man supposedly knows everything, sees everything, thinks for everyone, can do anything, is infallible in his behavior.

Such a belief about a man, and specifically about Stalin, was cultivated among us for many years. The objective of the present report is not a thorough evaluation of Stalin's life and activity. Concerning Stalin's merits, an entirely sufficient number of books, pamphlets and studies had already been written in his lifetime. Stalin's role of Stalin in the preparation and execution of the Socialist Revolution, in the Civil War, and in the fight for the construction of socialism in our country, is universally known. Everyone knows it well.

At present, we are concerned with a question which has immense importance for the Party now and for the future – with how the cult of the person of Stalin has been gradually growing, the cult which became at a certain specific stage the source of a whole series of exceedingly serious and grave perversions of Party principles, of Party democracy, of revolutionary legality.

Because not all as yet realize fully the practical consequences resulting from the cult of the individual, [or] the great harm caused by violation of the principle of collective Party direction and by the accumulation of immense and limitless power in the hands of one person, the Central Committee considers it absolutely necessary to make material pertaining to this matter available to the 20th Congress of the Communist Party of the Soviet Union.

Allow me first of all to remind you how severely the classics of Marxism-Leninism denounced every manifestation of the cult of the individual. In a letter to the German political worker Wilhelm Bloss, [Karl] Marx stated: "From my antipathy to any cult of the individual, I never made public during the existence of the [1st] International the numerous addresses from various countries which recognized my merits and which annoyed me. I did not even reply to them, except sometimes to rebuke their authors. [Fredrich] Engels and I first joined the secret society of Communists on the condition that everything making for superstitious worship of authority would be deleted from its statute. [Ferdinand] Lassalle subsequently did quite the opposite."

Sometime later Engels wrote: "Both Marx and I have always been against any public manifestation with regard to individuals, with the exception of cases when it had an important purpose. We most strongly opposed such manifestations which during our lifetime concerned us personally."

The great modesty of the genius of the Revolution, Vladimir Ilyich Lenin, is known. Lenin always stressed the role of the people as the creator of history, the directing and organizational roles of the Party as a living and creative organism, and also the role of the Central Committee.

Marxism does not negate the role of the leaders of the working class in directing the revolutionary liberation movement.

While ascribing great importance to the role of the leaders and organizers of the masses, Lenin at the same time mercilessly stigmatized every manifestation of the cult of the individual, inexorably combated [any] foreign-to-Marxism views about a "hero" and a "crowd," and countered all efforts to oppose a "hero" to the masses and to the people.

Lenin taught that the Party's strength depends on its indissoluble unity with the masses, on the fact that behind the Party follows the people – workers, peasants, and the intelligentsia. Lenin said, "Only he who believes in the people, [he] who submerges himself in the fountain of the living creativeness of the people, will win and retain power."

Lenin spoke with pride about the Bolshevik Communist Party as the leader and teacher of the people. He called for the presentation of all the most important questions before the opinion of knowledgeable workers, before the opinion of their Party. He said: "We believe in it, we see in it the wisdom, the honor, and the conscience of our epoch."

Lenin resolutely stood against every attempt aimed at belittling or weakening the directing role of the Party in the structure of the Soviet state. He worked out Bolshevik principles of Party direction and norms of Party life, stressing that the guiding principle of Party leadership is its collegiality. Already during the pre-Revolutionary years, Lenin called the Central Committee a collective of leaders and the guardian and interpreter of Party principles. "During the period between congresses," Lenin pointed out, "the Central Committee guards and interprets the principles of the Party."

Underlining the role of the Central Committee and its authority, Vladimir Ilyich pointed out: "Our Central Committee constituted itself as a closely centralized and highly authoritative group."

During Lenin's life the Central Committee was a real expression of collective leadership: of the Party and of the nation. Being a militant Marxist-revolutionist, always unyielding in matters of principle, Lenin never imposed his views upon his co-workers by force. He tried to convince. He patiently explained his opinions to others. Lenin always diligently saw to it that the norms of Party life were realized, that Party statutes were enforced, that Party congresses and Plenary sessions of the Central Committee took place at their proper intervals.

In addition to V. I. Lenin's great accomplishments for the victory of the working class and of the working peasants, for the victory of our Party and for the application of the ideas of scientific Communism to life, his acute mind expressed itself also in this. [Lenin] detected in Stalin in time those negative characteristics which resulted later in grave consequences. Fearing the future fate of the Party and of the Soviet nation, V. I. Lenin made a completely correct characterization of Stalin. He pointed out that it was necessary to consider transferring Stalin from the position of [Party] General Secretary because Stalin was excessively rude, did not have a proper attitude toward his comrades, and was capricious and abused his power.

In December 1922, in a letter to the Party Congress, Vladimir Ilyich wrote: "After taking over the position of General Secretary, comrade Stalin accumulated immeasurable power in his hands and I am not certain whether he will be always able to use this power with the required care."

This letter – a political document of tremendous importance, known in the Party's history as Lenin's "Testament" - was distributed among [you] delegates to [this] 20th Party Congress. You have read it and will undoubtedly read it again more than once. You might reflect on Lenin's plain words, in which expression is given to Vladimir Ilyich's anxiety concerning the Party, the people, the state, and the future direction of Party policy.

Vladimir Ilyich said:

"Stalin is excessively rude, and this defect, which can be freely tolerated in our midst and in contacts among us Communists, becomes a defect which cannot be tolerated in one holding the position of General Secretary. Because of this, I propose that the comrades consider the method by which Stalin would be removed from this position and by which another man would be selected for it, a man who, above all, would differ from Stalin in only one quality, namely, greater tolerance, greater loyalty, greater kindness and more considerate attitude toward the comrades, a less capricious temper, etc."

This document of Lenin's was made known to the delegates at the 13th Party Congress, who discussed the question of transferring Stalin from the position of General Secretary. The delegates declared themselves in favor of retaining Stalin in this post, hoping that he would heed Vladimir Ilyich's critical remarks and would be able to overcome the defects which caused Lenin serious anxiety.

Comrades! The Party Congress should become acquainted with two new documents, which confirm Stalin's character as already outlined by Vladimir Ilyich Lenin in his "Testament." These documents are a letter from Nadezhda Konstantinovna Krupskaya to [Lev] Kamenev, who was at that time head of the Politbiuro, and a personal letter from Vladimir Ilyich Lenin to Stalin.

I will now read these documents:

"LEV BORISOVICH!

"Because of a short letter which I had written in words dictated to me by Vladimir Ilyich by permission of the doctors, Stalin allowed himself yesterday an unusually rude outburst directed at me.

This is not my first day in the Party. During all these 30 years I have never heard one word of rudeness from any comrade. The Party's and Ilyich's business is no less dear to me than to Stalin. I need maximum self-control right now. What

15

one can and what one cannot discuss with Ilyich I know better than any doctor, because I know what makes him nervous and what does not. In any case I know [it] better than Stalin. I am turning to you and to Grigory [Zinoviev] as much closer comrades of V[ladimir] I[lyich]. I beg you to protect me from rude interference with my private life and from vile invectives and threats. I have no doubt what the Control Commission's unanimous decision [in this matter], with which Stalin sees fit to threaten me, will be. However I have neither strength nor time to waste on this foolish quarrel. And I am a human being and my nerves are strained to the utmost.

"N. KRUPSKAYA"

Nadezhda Konstantinovna wrote this letter on December 23, 1922. After two and a half months, in March 1923, Vladimir Ilyich Lenin sent Stalin the following letter:

"TO COMRADE STALIN (COPIES FOR: KAMENEV AND ZINOVIEV):

"Dear comrade Stalin!

"You permitted yourself a rude summons of my wife to the telephone and a rude reprimand of her. Despite the fact that she told you that she agreed to forget what was said, nevertheless Zinoviev and Kamenev heard about it from her. I have no intention to forget so easily that which is being done against me. I need not stress here that I consider as directed against me that which is being done against my wife. I ask you, therefore, that you weigh carefully whether you are agreeable to retracting your words and apologizing, or whether you prefer the severance of relations between us.

"SINCERELY: LENIN, MARCH 5, 1923

(Commotion in the hall.)

Comrades! I will not comment on these documents. They speak eloquently for themselves. Since Stalin could behave in this manner during Lenin's life, could thus behave toward Nadezhda Konstantinovna Krupskaya – whom the Party knows well and values highly as a loyal friend of Lenin and as an active fighter for the cause of the Party since its creation – we can easily imagine how Stalin treated other people. These negative characteristics of his developed steadily and during the last years acquired an absolutely insufferable character.

As later events have proven, Lenin's anxiety was justified. In the first period after Lenin's death, Stalin still paid attention to his advice, but later he began to disregard the serious admonitions of Vladimir Ilyich. When we analyze the practice of Stalin in regard to the direction of the Party and of the country, when we pause to consider everything which Stalin perpetrated, we must be convinced that Lenin's fears were justified. The negative characteristics of Stalin, which, in Lenin's time, were only incipient, transformed themselves during the last years into a grave abuse of power by Stalin, which caused untold harm to our Party.

We have to consider seriously and analyze correctly this matter in order that we may preclude any possibility of a repetition in any form whatever of what took place during the life of Stalin, who absolutely did not tolerate collegiality in leadership and in work, and who practiced brutal violence, not only toward everything which opposed him, but also toward that which seemed, to his capricious and despotic character, contrary to his concepts.

Stalin acted not through persuasion, explanation and patient cooperation with people, but by imposing his concepts and demanding absolute submission to his opinion. Whoever opposed these concepts or tried to prove his [own] viewpoint and the correctness of his [own] position was doomed to removal from the leadership collective and to subsequent moral and physical annihilation. This was especially true during the period following the 17th Party Congress, when many prominent Party leaders and rank-and-file Party workers, honest and dedicated to the cause of Communism, fell victim to

Stalin's despotism.

We must affirm that the Party fought a serious fight against the Trotskyites, rightists and bourgeois nationalists, and that it disarmed ideologically all the enemies of Leninism. This ideological fight was carried on successfully, as a result of which the Party became strengthened and tempered. Here Stalin played a positive role.

The Party led a great political-ideological struggle against those in its own ranks who proposed anti-Leninist theses, who represented a political line hostile to the Party and to the cause of socialism. This was a stubborn and a difficult fight but a necessary one, because the political line of both the Trotskyite-Zinovievite bloc and of the Bukharinites led actually toward the restoration of capitalism and toward capitulation to the world bourgeoisie. Let us consider for a moment what would have happened if in 1928-1929 the political line of right deviation had prevailed among us, or orientation toward "cotton-dress industrialization," or toward the kulak, etc. We would not now have a powerful heavy industry; we would not have the kolkhozes; we would find ourselves disarmed and weak in a capitalist encirclement.

It was for this reason that the Party led an inexorable ideological fight, explaining to all [its] members and to the non-Party masses the harm and the danger of the anti-Leninist proposals of the Trotskyite opposition and the rightist opportunists. And this great work of explaining the Party line bore fruit. Both the Trotskyites and the rightist opportunists were politically isolated. An overwhelming Party majority supported the Leninist line, and the Party was able to awaken and organize the working masses to apply the Leninist line and to build socialism.

A fact worth noting is that extreme repressive measures were not used against the Trotskyites, the Zinovievites, the Bukharinites, and others during the course of the furious ideological fight against them. The fight [in the 1920s] was on ideological grounds. But some years later, when socialism in our country was fundamentally constructed, when the exploiting classes were generally liquidated, when Soviet social structure had radically changed, when the social basis for political movements and groups hostile to the Party had violently contracted, when the ideological opponents of the Party were long since defeated politically – then repression directed against them began. It was precisely during this period (1935-1937-1938) that the practice of mass repression through the Government apparatus was born, first against the enemies of Leninism – Trotskyites, Zinovievites, Bukharinites, long since politically defeated by the Party – and subsequently also against many honest Communists, against those Party cadres who had borne the heavy load of the Civil War and the first and most difficult years of industrialization and collectivization, who had fought actively against the Trotskyites and the rightists for the Leninist Party line.

Stalin originated the concept "enemy of the people." This term automatically made it unnecessary that the ideological errors of a man or men engaged in a controversy be proven. It made possible the use of the cruelest repression, violating all norms of revolutionary legality, against anyone who in any way disagreed with Stalin, against those who were only suspected of hostile intent, against those who had bad reputations. The concept "enemy of the people" actually eliminated the possibility of any kind of ideological fight or the making of one's views known on this or that issue, even [issues] of a practical nature. On the whole, the only proof of guilt actually used, against all norms of current legal science, was the "confession" of the accused himself. As subsequent probing has proven, "confessions" were acquired through physical pressures against the accused. This led to glaring violations of revolutionary legality and to the fact that many entirely innocent individuals – [persons] who in the past had defended the Party line – became victims.

We must assert that, in regard to those persons who in

their time had opposed the Party line, there were often no sufficiently serious reasons for their physical annihilation. The formula "enemy of the people" was specifically introduced for the purpose of physically annihilating such individuals.

It is a fact that many persons who were later annihilated as enemies of the Party and people had worked with Lenin during his life. Some of these persons had made errors during Lenin's life, but, despite this, Lenin benefited by their work; he corrected them and he did everything possible to retain them in the ranks of the Party; he induced them to follow him.

In this connection the delegates to the Party Congress should familiarize themselves with an unpublished note by V. I. Lenin directed to the Central Committee's Politbiuro in October 1920. Outlining the duties of the [Party] Control Commission, Lenin wrote that the Commission should be transformed into a real "organ of Party and proletarian conscience."

"As a special duty of the Control Commission there is recommended a deep, individualized relationship with, and sometimes even a type of therapy for, the representatives of the so-called opposition – those who have experienced a psychological crisis because of failure in their Soviet or Party career. An effort should be made to quiet them, to explain the matter to them in a way used among comrades, to find for them (avoiding the method of issuing orders) a task for which they are psychologically fitted. Advice and rules relating to this matter are to be formulated by the Central Committee's Organizational Bureau, etc."

Everyone knows how irreconcilable Lenin was with the ideological enemies of Marxism, with those who deviated from the correct Party line. At the same time, however, Lenin, as is evident from the given document, in his practice of directing the Party demanded the most intimate Party contact with people who had shown indecision or temporary non-conformity with the Party line, but whom it was possible to return to the Party path. Lenin advised that such people should be patiently educated without the application of extreme methods.

Lenin's wisdom in dealing with people was evident in his work with cadres.

An entirely different relationship with people characterized Stalin. Lenin's traits – patient work with people, stubborn and painstaking education of them, the ability to induce people to follow him without using compulsion, but rather through the ideological influence on them of the whole collective – were entirely foreign to Stalin. He discarded the Leninist method of convincing and educating, he abandoned the method of ideological struggle for that of administrative violence, mass repressions and terror. He acted on an increasingly larger scale and more stubbornly through punitive organs, at the same time often violating all existing norms of morality and of Soviet laws.

Arbitrary behavior by one person encouraged and permitted arbitrariness in others. Mass arrests and deportations of many thousands of people, execution without trial and without normal investigation created conditions of insecurity, fear and even desperation.

This, of course, did not contribute toward unity of the Party ranks and of all strata of working people, but, on the contrary, brought about annihilation and the expulsion from the Party of workers who were loyal but inconvenient to Stalin.

Our Party fought for the implementation of Lenin's plans for the construction of socialism. This was an ideological fight. Had Leninist principles been observed during the course of this fight, had the Party's devotion to principles been skillfully combined with a keen and solicitous concern for people, had they not been repelled and wasted but rather drawn to our side, we certainly would not have had such a brutal violation of revolutionary legality and many thousands of people would not have fallen victim to the method of terror. Extraordinary methods would then have been resorted to only

21

against those people who had in fact committed criminal acts against the Soviet system.

Let us recall some historical facts.

In the days before the October Revolution, two members of the Central Committee of the Bolshevik Party – Kamenev and Zinoviev – declared themselves against Lenin's plan for an armed uprising. In addition, on October 18 they published in the Menshevik newspaper, *Novaya Zhizn*, a statement declaring that the Bolsheviks were making preparations for an uprising and that they considered it adventuristic. Kamenev and Zinoviev thus disclosed to the enemy the decision of the Central Committee to stage the uprising, and that the uprising had been organized to take place within the very near future.

This was treason against the Party and against the Revolution. In this connection, V. I. Lenin wrote: "Kamenev and Zinoviev revealed the decision of the Central Committee of their Party on the armed uprising to [Mikhail] Rodzyanko and [Alexander] Kerensky.... He put before the Central Committee the question of Zinoviev's and Kamenev's expulsion from the Party.

However, after the Great Socialist October Revolution, as is known, Zinoviev and Kamenev were given leading positions. Lenin put them in positions in which they carried out most responsible Party tasks and participated actively in the work of the leading Party and Soviet organs. It is known that Zinoviev and Kamenev committed a number of other serious errors during Lenin's life. In his "Testament" Lenin warned that "Zinoviev's and Kamenev's October episode was of course not an accident." But Lenin did not pose the question of their arrest and certainly not their shooting.

Or, let us take the example of the Trotskyites. At present, after a sufficiently long historical period, we can speak about the fight with the Trotskyites with complete calm and can analyze this matter with sufficient objectivity. After all, around

Trotsky were people whose origin cannot by any means be traced to bourgeois society. Part of them belonged to the Party intelligentsia and a certain part were recruited from among the workers. We can name many individuals who, in their time, joined the Trotskyites; however, these same individuals took an active part in the workers' movement before the Revolution, during the Socialist October Revolution itself, and also in the consolidation of the victory of this greatest of revolutions. Many of them broke with Trotskyism and returned to Leninist positions. Was it necessary to annihilate such people? We are deeply convinced that, had Lenin lived, such an extreme method would not have been used against any of them.

Such are only a few historical facts. But can it be said that Lenin did not decide to use even the most severe means against enemies of the Revolution when this was actually necessary? No; no one can say this. Vladimir Ilyich demanded uncompromising dealings with the enemies of the Revolution and of the working class and when necessary resorted ruthlessly to such methods. You will recall only V. I. Lenin's fight with the Socialist Revolutionary organizers of the anti-Soviet uprising, with the counterrevolutionary kulaks in 1918 and with others, when Lenin without hesitation used the most extreme methods against the enemies. Lenin used such methods, however, only against actual class enemies and not against those who blunder, who err, and whom it was possible to lead through ideological influence and even retain in the leadership. Lenin used severe methods only in the most necessary cases, when the exploiting classes were still in existence and were vigorously opposing the Revolution, when the struggle for survival was decidedly assuming the sharpest forms, even including a Civil War.

Stalin, on the other hand, used extreme methods and mass repressions at a time when the Revolution was already victorious, when the Soviet state was strengthened, when the exploiting classes were already liquidated and socialist relations were rooted solidly in all phases of national economy, when our Party was politically consolidated and had strengthened itself both numerically and ideologically.

It is clear that here Stalin showed in a whole series of cases his intolerance, his brutality and his abuse of power. Instead of proving his political correctness and mobilizing the masses, he often chose the path of repression and physical annihilation, not only against actual enemies, but also against individuals who had not committed any crimes against the Party and the Soviet Government. Here we see no wisdom but only a demonstration of the brutal force which had once so alarmed V. I. Lenin.

Lately, especially after the unmasking of the Beria gang, the Central Committee looked into a series of matters fabricated by this gang. This revealed a very ugly picture of brutal willfulness connected with the incorrect behavior of Stalin. As facts prove, Stalin, using his unlimited power, allowed himself many abuses, acting in the name of the Central Committee, not asking for the opinion of the Committee members nor even of the members of the Central Committee's Politbiuro; often he did not inform them about his personal decisions concerning very important Party and government matters.

Considering the question of the cult of an individual, we must first of all show everyone what harm this caused to the interests of our Party.

Vladimir Ilyich Lenin had always stressed the Party's role and significance in the direction of the socialist government of workers and peasants; he saw in this the chief precondition for a successful building of socialism in our country. Pointing to the great responsibility of the Bolshevik Party, as ruling Party of the Soviet state, Lenin called for the most meticulous observance of all norms of Party life; he called for the realization of the principles of collegiality in the direction of the Party and the state.

Collegiality of leadership flows from the very nature of our Party, a Party built on the principles of democratic centralism. "This means," said Lenin, "that all Party matters are accomplished by all Party members – directly or through representatives – who, without any exceptions, are subject to the same rules; in addition, all administrative members, all directing collegia, all holders of Party positions are elective, they must account for their activities and are recallable."

It is known that Lenin himself offered an example of the most careful observance of these principles. There was no matter so important that Lenin himself decided it without asking for advice and approval of the majority of the Central Committee members or of the members of the Central Committee's Politbiuro. In the most difficult period for our Party and our country, Lenin considered it necessary regularly to convoke Congresses, Party Conferences and Plenary sessions of the Central Committee at which all the most important questions were discussed and where resolutions, carefully worked out by the collective of leaders, were approved.

We can recall, for an example, the year 1918 when the country was threatened by the attack of the imperialistic interventionists. In this situation the 7th Party Congress was convened in order to discuss a vitally important matter which could not be postponed – the matter of peace. In 1919, while the Civil War was raging, the 8th Party Congress convened which adopted a new Party program, decided such important matters as the relationship with the peasant masses, the organization of the Red Army, the leading role of the Party in the work of the soviets, the correction of the social composition of the Party, and other matters. In 1920 the 9th Party Congress was convened which laid down guiding principles pertaining to the Party's work in the sphere of economic construction. In 1921 the 10th Party Congress accepted Lenin's New Economic Policy and the historic resolution called "On Party Unity."

During Lenin's life, Party congresses were convened regularly; always, when a radical turn in the development of the Party and the country took place, Lenin considered it absolutely necessary that the Party discuss at length all the basic matters pertaining to internal and foreign policy and to questions bearing on the development of Party and government.

It is very characteristic that Lenin addressed to the Party Congress as the highest Party organ his last articles, letters and remarks. During the period between congresses, the Central Committee of the Party, acting as the most authoritative leading collective, meticulously observed the principles of the Party and carried out its policy.

So it was during Lenin's life. Were our Party's holy Leninist principles observed after the death of Vladimir Ilyich?

Whereas, during the first few years after Lenin's death, Party Congresses and Central Committee Plenums took place more or less regularly, later, when Stalin began increasingly to abuse his power, these principles were brutally violated. This was especially evident during the last 15 years of his life. Was it a normal situation when over 13 years elapsed between the 18th and 19th Party Congresses, years during which our Party and our country had experienced so many important events? These events demanded categorically that the Party should have passed resolutions pertaining to the country's defense during the [Great] Patriotic War and to peacetime construction after the war.

Even after the end of the war a Congress was not convened for over seven years. Central Committee Plenums were hardly ever called. It should be sufficient to mention that during all the years of the Patriotic War not a single Central Committee Plenum took place. It is true that there was an attempt to call a Central Committee Plenum in October 1941, when Central Committee members from the whole country were called to Moscow. They waited two days for the opening of the Plenum, but in vain. Stalin did not even want to meet and talk to the Central Committee members. This fact shows how demoralized Stalin was in the first months of the war and how haughtily and disdainfully he treated the Central Committee members.

In practice, Stalin ignored the norms of Party life and trampled on the Leninist principle of collective Party leadership.

Stalin's willfulness vis a vis the Party and its Central Committee became fully evident after the 17th Party Congress, which took place in 1934.

Having at its disposal numerous data showing brutal willfulness toward Party cadres, the Central Committee has created a Party commission under the control of the Central Committee's Presidium. It has been charged with investigating what made possible mass repressions against the majority of the Central Committee members and candidates elected at the 17th Congress of the All-Union Communist Party (Bolsheviks).

The commission has become acquainted with a large quantity of materials in the NKVD archives and with other documents. It has established many facts pertaining to the fabrication of cases against Communists, to false accusations, [and] to glaring abuses of socialist legality, which resulted in the death of innocent people. It became apparent that many Party, Soviet and economic activists who in 1937-1938 were branded "enemies" were actually never enemies, spies, wreckers, etc., but were always honest Communists. They were merely stigmatized [as enemies]. Often, no longer able to bear barbaric tortures, they charged themselves (at the order of the investigative judges/falsifiers) with all kinds of grave and unlikely crimes.

The commission has presented to the Central Committee's Presidium lengthy and documented materials pertaining to mass repressions against the delegates to the 17th Party Congress and against members of the Central Committee elected at that Congress. These materials have been studied by the Presidium..

It was determined that of the 139 members and candidates of the Central Committee who were elected at the

17th Congress, 98 persons, i.e., 70 per cent, were arrested and shot (mostly in 1937-1938). (Indignation in the hall.) What was the composition of the delegates to the 17th Congress? It is known that 80 per cent of the voting participants of the 17th Congress joined the Party during the years of conspiracy before the Revolution and during the Civil War, i.e. meaning before 1921. By social origin the basic mass of the delegates to the Congress were workers (60 per cent of the voting members).

For this reason, it is inconceivable that a Congress so composed could have elected a Central Committee in which a majority [of the members] would prove to be enemies of the Party. The only reasons why 70 per cent of the Central Committee members and candidates elected at the 17th Congress were branded as enemies of the Party and of the people were because honest Communists were slandered, accusations against them were fabricated, and revolutionary legality was gravely undermined.

The same fate met not only Central Committee members but also the majority of the delegates to the 17th Party Congress. Of 1,966 delegates with either voting or advisory rights, 1,108 persons were arrested on charges of anti-revolutionary crimes, i.e., decidedly more than a majority. This very fact shows how absurd, wild and contrary to common sense were the charges of counterrevolutionary crimes made out, as we now see, against a majority of participants at the 17th Party Congress.

(Indignation in the hall.)

We should recall that the 17th Party Congress is known historically as the Congress of Victors. Delegates to the Congress were active participants in the building of our socialist state; many of them suffered and fought for Party interests during the pre-Revolutionary years in the conspiracy and at the civil-war fronts; they fought their enemies valiantly and often nervelessly looked into the face of death.

How, then, can we believe that such people could prove to be "two-faced" and had joined the camps of the enemies of socialism during the era after the political liquidation of Zinovievites, Trotskyites and rightists and after the great accomplishments of socialist construction? This was the result of the abuse of power by Stalin, who began to use mass terror against Party cadres.

What is the reason that mass repressions against activists increased more and more after the 17th Party Congress? It was because at that time Stalin had so elevated himself above the Party and above the nation that he ceased to consider either the Central Committee or the Party.

Stalin still reckoned with the opinion of the collective before the 17th Congress. After the complete political liquidation of the Trotskyites, Zinovievites and Bukharinites, however, when the Party had achieved unity, Stalin to an ever greater degree stopped considering the members of the Party's Central Committee and even the members of the Politbiuro. Stalin thought that now he could decide all things alone and that all he needed were statisticians. He treated all others in such a way that they could only listen to him and praise him.

After the criminal murder of Sergey M. Kirov, mass repressions and brutal acts of violation of socialist legality began. On the evening of December 1, 1934 on Stalin's initiative (without the approval of the Politbiuro –which was given two days later, casually), the Secretary of the Presidium of the Central Executive Committee, [Abel] Yenukidze, signed the following directive:

"1. Investigative agencies are directed to speed up the cases of those accused of the preparation or execution of acts of terror.

"2. Judicial organs are directed not to hold up the execution of death sentences pertaining to crimes of this category in order to consider the possibility of pardon, because

29

the Presidium of the Central Executive Committee of the USSR does not consider as possible the receiving of petitions of this sort.

"3. The organs of the Commissariat of Internal Affairs [NKVD] are directed to execute the death sentences against criminals of the above-mentioned category immediately after the passage of sentences."

This directive became the basis for mass acts of abuse against socialist legality. During many of the fabricated court cases, the accused were charged with "the preparation" of terroristic acts; this deprived them of any possibility that their cases might be re-examined, even when they stated before the court that their "confessions" were secured by force, and when, in a convincing manner, they disproved the accusations against them.

It must be asserted that to this day the circumstances surrounding Kirov's murder hide many things which are inexplicable and mysterious and demand a most careful examination. There are reasons for the suspicion that the killer of Kirov, [Leonid] Nikolayev, was assisted by someone from among the people whose duty it was to protect the person of Kirov.

A month and a half before the killing, Nikolayev was arrested on the grounds of suspicious behavior but he was released and not even searched. It is an unusually suspicious circumstance that when the Chekist assigned to protect Kirov was being brought for an interrogation, on December 2, 1934, he was killed in a car "accident" in which no other occupants of the car were harmed. After the murder of Kirov, top functionaries of the Leningrad NKVD were given very light sentences, but in 1937 they were shot. We can assume that they were shot in order to cover up the traces of the organizers of Kirov's killing.

(Movement in the hall.)

Mass repressions grew tremendously from the end of 1936 after a telegram from Stalin and [Andrey] Zhdanov, dated from Sochi on September 25, 1936, was addressed to [Lazar] Kaganovich, [Vyacheslav] Molotov and other members of the Politbiuro. The content of the telegram was as follows:

"We deem it absolutely necessary and urgent that comrade [Nikolay] Yezhov be nominated to the post of People's Commissar for Internal Affairs. [Genrikh] Yagoda definitely has proven himself incapable of unmasking the Trotskyite-Zinovievite bloc. The OGPU is four years behind in this matter. This is noted by all Party workers and by the majority of the representatives of the NKVD."

Strictly speaking, we should stress that Stalin did not meet with and, therefore, could not know the opinion of Party workers.

This Stalinist formulation that the "NKVD is four years behind" in applying mass repression and that there is a necessity for "catching up" with the neglected work directly pushed the NKVD workers on the path of mass arrests and executions.

We should state that this formulation was also forced on the February-March Plenary session of the Central Committee of the All-Union Communist Party (Bolsheviks) in 1937. The Plenary resolution approved it on the basis of Yezhov's report, "Lessons flowing from the harmful activity, diversion and espionage of the Japanese-German-Trotskyite agents," stating:

"The Plenum of the Central Committee of the All-Union Communist Party (Bolsheviks) considers that all facts revealed during the investigation into the matter of an anti-Soviet Trotskyite center and of its followers in the provinces show that the People's Commissariat of Internal Affairs has fallen behind at least four years in the attempt to unmask these most inexorable enemies of the people.

The mass repressions at this time were made under the slogan of a fight against the Trotskyites. Did the Trotskyites at this time actually constitute such a danger to our Party and to the Soviet state? We should recall that in 1927, on the eve of the 15th Party Congress, only some 4,000 [Party] votes were cast for the Trotskyite-Zinovievite opposition while there were 724,000 for the Party line. During the 10 years which passed between the 15th Party Congress and the February-March Central Committee Plenum, Trotskyism was completely disarmed. Many former Trotskyites changed their former views and worked in the various sectors building socialism. It is clear that in the situation of socialist victory there was no basis for mass terror in the country.

Stalin's report at the February-March Central Committee Plenum in 1937, "Deficiencies of Party work and methods for the liquidation of the Trotskyites and of other two-facers," contained an attempt at theoretical justification of the mass terror policy under the pretext that class war must allegedly sharpen as we march forward toward socialism. Stalin asserted that both history and Lenin taught him this.

Actually Lenin taught that the application of revolutionary violence is necessitated by the resistance of the exploiting classes, and this referred to the era when the exploiting classes existed and were powerful. As soon as the nation's political situation had improved, when in January 1920 the Red Army took Rostov and thus won a most important victory over [General A. I.] Denikin, Lenin instructed [Felix] Dzerzhinsky to stop mass terror and to abolish the death penalty. Lenin justified this important political move of the Soviet state in the following manner in his report at the session of the All-Union Central Executive Committee on February 2, 1920:

"We were forced to use terror because of the terror practiced by the Entente, when strong world powers threw their hordes against us, not avoiding any type of conduct. We would not have lasted two days had we not answered these attempts of officers and White Guardists in a merciless fashion; this meant the use of terror, but this was forced upon us by the terrorist methods of the Entente.

"But as soon as we attained a decisive victory, even before the end of the war, immediately after taking Rostov, we gave up the use of the death penalty and thus proved that we intend to execute our own program in the manner that we promised. We say that the application of violence flows out of the decision to smother the exploiters, the big landowners and the capitalists; as soon as this was accomplished we gave up the use of all extraordinary methods. We have proved this in practice."

Stalin deviated from these clear and plain precepts of Lenin. Stalin put the Party and the NKVD up to the use of mass terror when the exploiting classes had been liquidated in our country and when there were no serious reasons for the use of extraordinary mass terror.

This terror was actually directed not at the remnants of the defeated exploiting classes but against the honest workers of the Party and of the Soviet state; against them were made lying, slanderous and absurd accusations concerning "two-facedness," "espionage," "sabotage," preparation of fictitious "plots," etc.

At the February-March Central Committee Plenum in 1937 many members actually questioned the rightness of the established course regarding mass repressions under the pretext of combating "two-facedness."

Comrade [Pavel] Postyshev most ably expressed these doubts. He said:

"I have philosophized that the severe years of fighting have passed. Party members who have lost their backbones have broken down or have joined the camp of the enemy; healthy elements have fought for the Party. These were the years of industrialization and collectivization. I never thought it possible that after this severe era had passed Karpov and people like him would find themselves in the camp of the enemy.

Karpov was a worker in the Ukrainian Central Committee whom Postyshev knew well.) And now, according to the testimony, it appears that Karpov was recruited in 1934 by the Trotskyites. I personally do not believe that in 1934 an honest Party member who had trod the long road of unrelenting fight against enemies for the Party and for socialism would now be in the camp of the enemies. I do not believe it.... I cannot imagine how it would be possible to travel with the Party during the difficult years and then, in 1934, join the Trotskyites. It is an odd thing...."

(Movement in the hall.)

Using Stalin's formulation, namely, that the closer we are to socialism the more enemies we will have, and using the resolution of the February-March Central Committee Plenum passed on the basis of Yezhov's report, the provocateurs who had infiltrated the state-security organs together with conscienceless careerists began to protect with the Party name the mass terror against Party cadres, cadres of the Soviet state, and ordinary Soviet citizens. It should suffice to say that the number of arrests based on charges of counterrevolutionary crimes had grown ten times between 1936 and 1937.

It is known that brutal willfulness was practiced against leading Party workers. The [relevant] Party statute, approved at the 17th Party Congress, was based on Leninist principles expressed at the 10th Party Congress. It stated that, in order to apply an extreme method such as exclusion from the Party against a Central Committee member, against a Central Committee candidate or against a member of the Party Control Commission, "it is necessary to call a Central Committee Plenum and to invite to the Plenum all Central Committee candidate members and all members of the Party Control Commission"; only if two-thirds of the members of such a general assembly of responsible Party leaders found it necessary, only then could a Central Committee member or candidate be expelled.

The majority of those Central Committee's members and candidates who were elected at the 17th Congress and arrested in 1937-1938 were expelled from the Party illegally through brutal abuse of the Party statute, because the question of their expulsion was never studied at the Central Committee Plenum.

Now, when the cases of some of these so-called "spies" and "saboteurs" were examined, it was found that all their cases were fabricated. The confessions of guilt of many of those arrested and charged with enemy activity were gained with the help of cruel and inhuman tortures.

At the same time, Stalin, as we have been informed by members of the Politbiuro of that time, did not show them the statements of many accused political activists when they retracted their confessions before the military tribunal and asked for an objective examination of their cases. There were many such declarations, and Stalin doubtless knew of them.

The Central Committee considers it absolutely necessary to inform the Congress of many such fabricated "cases" against the members of the Party's Central Committee elected at the 17th Party Congress.

An example of vile provocation, of odious falsification and of criminal violation of revolutionary legality is the case of the former candidate for the Central Committee Politbiuro, one of the most eminent workers of the Party and of the Soviet Government, comrade [Robert] Eikhe, who had been a Party member since 1905.

(Commotion in the hall.)

Comrade Eikhe was arrested on April 29, 1938 on the basis of slanderous materials, without the sanction of the [State] Prosecutor of the USSR. This was finally received 15 months after the arrest.

The investigation of Eikhe's case was made in a manner which most brutally violated Soviet legality and was accompanied by willfulness and falsification.

Under torture, Eikhe was forced to sign a protocol of his confession prepared in advance by the investigative judges. In it, he and several other eminent Party workers were accused of anti-Soviet activity.

On October 1, 1939 Eikhe sent his declaration to Stalin in which he categorically denied his guilt and asked for an examination of his case. In the declaration he wrote: "There is no more bitter misery than to sit in the jail of a government for which I have always fought."

A second declaration of Eikhe has been preserved, which he sent to Stalin on October 27, 1939. In it [Eikhe] cited facts very convincingly and countered the slanderous accusations made against him, arguing that this provocatory accusation was on one hand the work of real Trotskyites whose arrests he had sanctioned as First Secretary of the West Siberian Regional Party Committee and who conspired in order to take revenge on him, and, on the other hand, the result of the base falsification of materials by the investigative judges.

Eikhe wrote in his declaration:

"... On October 25 of this year I was informed that the investigation in my case has been concluded and I was given access to the materials of this investigation. Had I been guilty of only one hundredth of the crimes with which I am charged, I would not have dared to send you this pre-execution declaration. However I have not been guilty of even one of the things with which I am charged and my heart is clean of even the shadow of baseness. I have never in my life told you a word of falsehood, and now, finding both feet in the grave, I am still not lying. My whole case is a typical example of provocation, slander and violation of the elementary basis of revolutionary legality....

"... The confessions which were made part of my file are not only absurd but contain slander toward the Central Committee of the All-Union Communist Party (Bolsheviks) and toward the Council of People's Commissars. [This is] because correct resolutions of the Central Committee of the All-Union Communist Party (Bolsheviks) and of the Council of People's Commissars which were not made on my initiative and [were promulgated] without my participation are presented as hostile acts of counterrevolutionary organizations made at my suggestion.

"I am now alluding to the most disgraceful part of my life and to my really grave guilt against the Party and against you. This is my confession of counterrevolutionary activity.... The case is as follows: Not being able to suffer the tortures to which I was submitted by [Z.] Ushakov and Nikolayev – especially by the former, who utilized the knowledge that my broken ribs have not properly mended and have caused me great pain – I have been forced to accuse myself and others.

"The majority of my confession has been suggested or dictated by Ushakov. The rest is my reconstruction of NKVD materials from Western Siberia for which I assumed all responsibility. If some part of the story which Ushakov fabricated and which I signed did not properly hang together, I was forced to sign another variation. The same thing was done to [Moisey] Rukhimovich, who was at first designated as a member of the reserve net and whose name later was removed without telling me anything about it. The same also was done with the leader of the reserve net, supposedly created by Bukharin in 1935. At first I wrote my [own] name in, and then I was instructed to insert [Valery] Mezhlauk's. There were other similar incidents.

"... I am asking and begging you that you again examine my case, and this not for the purpose of sparing me but in order to unmask the vile provocation which, like a snake, wound itself around many persons in a great degree due to my meanness and criminal slander. I have never betrayed you or the Party. I know that I perish because of vile and mean work of enemies of the Party and of the people, who have fabricated the provocation against me."

It would appear that such an important declaration was worth an examination by the Central Committee. This, however, was not done. The declaration was transmitted to Beria while the terrible maltreatment of the Politbiuro candidate, comrade Eikhe, continued.

On February 2, 1940, Eikhe was brought before the court. Here he did not confess any guilt and said as follows:

"In all the so-called confessions of mine there is not one letter written by me with the exception of my signatures under the protocols, which were forced from me. I have made my confession under pressure from the investigative judge, who from the time of my arrest tormented me. After that I began to write all this nonsense.... The most important thing for me is to tell the court, the Party and Stalin that I am not guilty. I have never been guilty of any conspiracy. I will die believing in the truth of Party policy as I have believed in it during my whole life."

On February 4, Eikhe was shot.

(Indignation in the hall.)

It has been definitely established now that Eikhe's case was fabricated. He has been rehabilitated posthumously.

Comrade [Yan] Rudzutak, a candidate-member of the Politbiuro, a member of the Party since 1905 who spent 10 years in a Tsarist hard-labor camp, completely retracted in court the confession forced from him. The protocol of the session of the Collegium of the Supreme Military Court contains the following statement by Rudzutak:

"... The only plea which [the defendant] places before the court is that the Central Committee of the All-Union Communist Party (Bolsheviks) be informed that there is in the NKVD an as yet not liquidated center which is craftily manufacturing cases, which forces innocent persons to confess.

There is no opportunity to prove one's non-participation in crimes to which the confessions of various persons testify. The investigative methods are such that they force people to lie and to slander entirely innocent persons in addition to those who already stand accused. [The defendant] asks the Court that he be allowed to inform the Central Committee of the All-Union Communist Party (Bolsheviks) about all this in writing. He assures the Court that he personally had never any evil designs in regard to the policy of our Party because he has always agreed with Party policy concerning all spheres of economic and cultural activity."

This declaration of Rudzutak was ignored, despite the fact that Rudzutak was in his time the head of the Central Control Commission– which had been called into being, in accordance with Lenin's conception, for the purpose of fighting for Party unity. In this manner fell the head of this highly authoritative Party organ, a victim of brutal willfulness. He was not even called before the Politbiuro because Stalin did not want to talk to him. Sentence was pronounced on him in 20 minutes and he was shot.

(Indignation in the hall.)

After careful examination of the case in 1955, it was established that the accusation against Rudzutak was false and that it was based on slanderous materials. Rudzutak has been rehabilitated posthumously.

The way in which the former NKVD workers manufactured various fictitious "anti-Soviet centers" and "blocs" with the help of provocatory methods is seen from the confession of comrade Rozenblum, a Party member since 1906, who was arrested in 1937 by the Leningrad NKVD.

During the examination in 1955 of the Komarov case, Rozenblum revealed the following fact: When Rozenblum was arrested in 1937, he was subjected to terrible torture during which he was ordered to confess false information concerning

39

himself and other persons. He was then brought to the office of [Leonid] Zakovsky, who offered him freedom on condition that he make before the court a false confession fabricated in 1937 by the NKVD concerning "sabotage, espionage and diversion in a terroristic center in Leningrad." (Movement in the hall.) With unbelievable cynicism, Zakovsky told about the vile "mechanism" for the crafty creation of fabricated "anti-Soviet plots."

"In order to illustrate it to me," stated Rozenblum, "Zakovsky gave me several possible variants of the organization of this center and of its branches. After he detailed the organization to me, Zakovsky told me that the NKVD would prepare the case of this center, remarking that the trial would be public. Before the court were to be brought 4 or 5 members of this center: [Mikhail] Chudov, [Fyodor] Ugarov, [Pyotr] Smorodin, [Boris] Pozern, Chudov's wife [Liudmilla] Shaposhnikova and others together with 2 or 3 members from the branches of this center....

"... The case of the Leningrad center has to be built solidly, and for this reason witnesses are needed. Social origin (of course, in the past) and the Party standing of the witness will play more than a small role. "'You, yourself,' said Zakovsky, 'will not need to invent anything. The NKVD will prepare for you a ready outline for every branch of the center. You will have to study it carefully, and remember well all questions the Court might ask and their answers. This case will be ready in four or five months, perhaps in half a year. During all this time you will be preparing yourself so that you will not compromise the investigation and yourself. Your future will depend on how the trial goes and on its results. If you begin to lie and to testify falsely, blame yourself. If you manage to endure it, you will save your head and we will feed and clothe you at the Government's cost until your death.'"

This is the kind of vile thing practiced then.

(Movement in the hall.)

Even more widely was the falsification of cases practiced in the provinces. The NKVD headquarters of the Sverdlov Province "discovered" a so-called "Ural uprising staff" – an organ of the bloc of rightists, Trotskyites, Socialist Revolutionaries, and church leaders – whose chief supposedly was the Secretary of the Sverdlov Provincial Party Committee and member of the Central Committee, All-Union Communist Party (Bolsheviks), [Ivan] Kabakov, who had been a Party member since 1914. Investigative materials of that time show that in almost all regions, provinces and republics there supposedly existed "rightist Trotskyite, espionage-terror and diversionary-sabotage organizations and centers" and that the heads of such organizations as a rule – for no known reason – were First Secretaries of provincial or republican Communist Party committees or Central Committees.

Many thousands of honest and innocent Communists have died as a result of this monstrous falsification of such "cases," as a result of the fact that all kinds of slanderous "confessions" were accepted, and as a result of the practice of forcing accusations against oneself and others. In the same manner were fabricated the "cases" against eminent Party and state workers – [Stanislav] Kosior, [Vlas] Chubar, [Pavel] Postyshev, [Alexander] Kosarev, and others.

In those years repressions on a mass scale were applied which were based on nothing tangible and which resulted in heavy cadre losses to the Party.

The vicious practice was condoned of having the NKVD prepare lists of persons whose cases were under the jurisdiction of the Military Collegium and whose sentences were prepared in advance. Yezhov would send these [execution] lists to Stalin personally for his approval of the proposed punishment. In 1937-1938, 383 such lists containing the names of many thousands of Party, Soviet, Komsomol, Army, and economic workers were sent to Stalin. He approved these lists.

A large part of these cases are being reviewed now. A

great many are being voided because they were baseless and falsified. Suffice it to say that from 1954 to the present time the Military Collegium of the Supreme Court has rehabilitated 7,679 persons, many of whom have been rehabilitated posthumously.

Mass arrests of Party, Soviet, economic and military workers caused tremendous harm to our country and to the cause of socialist advancement.

Mass repressions had a negative influence on the moral-political condition of the Party, created a situation of uncertainty, contributed to the spreading of unhealthy suspicion, and sowed distrust among Communists. All sorts of slanderers and careerists were active.

Resolutions of the January, 1938 Central Committee Plenum brought some measure of improvement to Party organizations. However, widespread repression also existed in 1938.

Only because our Party has at its disposal such great moral-political strength was it possible for it to survive the difficult events in 1937-1938 and to educate new cadres. There is, however, no doubt that our march forward toward socialism and toward the preparation of the country's defense would have been much more successful were it not for the tremendous loss in the cadres suffered as a result of the baseless and false mass repressions in 1937-1938.

We are accusing Yezhov justly for the degenerate practices of 1937. But we have to answer these questions: Could Yezhov have arrested Kosior, for instance, without Stalin's knowledge? Was there an exchange of opinions or a Politbiuro decision concerning this?

No, there was not, as there was none regarding other cases of this type. Could Yezhov have decided such important matters as the fate of such eminent Party figures?

No, it would be a display of naiveté to consider this the

work of Yezhov alone. It is clear that these matters were decided by Stalin, and that without his orders and his sanction Yezhov could not have done this.

We have examined these cases and have rehabilitated Kosior, Rudzutak, Postyshev, Kosarev and others. For what causes were they arrested and sentenced? Our review of evidence shows that there was no reason for this. They, like many others, were arrested without prosecutorial knowledge.

In such a situation, there is no need for any sanction, for what sort of a sanction could there be when Stalin decided everything? He was the chief prosecutor in these cases. Stalin not only agreed to arrest orders but issued them on his own initiative. We must say this so that the delegates to the Congress can clearly undertake and themselves assess this and draw the proper conclusions.

Facts prove that many abuses were made on Stalin's orders without reckoning with any norms of Party and Soviet legality. Stalin was a very distrustful man, sickly suspicious. We know this from our work with him. He could look at a man and say: "Why are your eyes so shifty today?" or "Why are you turning so much today and avoiding to look me directly in the eyes?" The sickly suspicion created in him a general distrust even toward eminent Party workers whom he had known for years. Everywhere and in everything he saw "enemies," "two-facers" and "spies." Possessing unlimited power, he indulged in great willfulness and stifled people morally as well as physically. A situation was created where one could not express one's own volition.

When Stalin said that one or another should be arrested, it was necessary to accept on faith that he was an "enemy of the people." Meanwhile, Beria's gang, which ran the organs of state security, outdid itself in proving the guilt of the arrested and the truth of materials which it falsified. And what proofs were offered? The confessions of the arrested, and the investigative judges accepted these "confessions." And how is it possible that a person confesses to crimes which he has not committed? Only in one way –because of the application of physical methods of pressuring him, tortures, bringing him to a state of unconsciousness, deprivation of his judgment, taking away of his human dignity. In this manner were "confessions" acquired.

The wave of mass arrests began to recede in 1939. When the leaders of territorial Party organizations began to accuse NKVD workers of using methods of physical pressure on the arrested, Stalin dispatched a coded telegram on January 20, 1939 to the committee secretaries of provinces and regions, to the central committees of republican Communist parties, to the [republican] People's Commissars of Internal Affairs and to the heads of NKVD organizations. This telegram stated:

"The Central Committee of the All-Union Communist Party (Bolsheviks) explains that the application of methods of physical pressure in NKVD practice is permissible from 1937 on in accordance with permission of the Central Committee of the All-Union Communist Party (Bolsheviks) ... It is known that all bourgeois intelligence services use methods of physical influence against representatives of the socialist proletariat and that they use them in their most scandalous forms.

"The question arises as to why the socialist intelligence service should be more humanitarian against the mad agents of the bourgeoisie, against the deadly enemies of the working class and of kolkhoz workers. The Central Committee of the All-Union Communist Party (Bolsheviks) considers that physical pressure should still be used obligatorily, as an exception applicable to known and obstinate enemies of the people, as a method both justifiable and appropriate."

Thus, Stalin had sanctioned in the name of the Central Committee of the All-Union Communist Party (Bolsheviks) the most brutal violation of socialist legality, torture and oppression, which led as we have seen to the slandering and to the self-accusation of innocent people.

Not long ago – only several days before the present Congress – we called to the Central Committee Presidium session and interrogated the investigative judge Rodos, who in his time investigated and interrogated Kosior, Chubar and Kosarev. He is a vile person, with the brain of a bird, and completely degenerate morally. It was this man who was deciding the fate of prominent Party workers. He also was making judgments concerning the politics in these matters, because, having established their "crime," he thereby provided materials from which important political implications could be drawn.

The question arises whether a man with such an intellect could–by himelf–have conducted his investigations in a manner proving the guilt of people such as Kosior and others. No, he could not have done it without proper directives. At the Central Committee Presidium session he told us: "I was told that Kosior and Chubar were people's enemies and for this reason I, as an investigative judge, had to make them confess that they were enemies."

(Indignation in the hall.)

He would do this only through long tortures, which he did, receiving detailed instructions from Beria. We must say that at the Central Committee Presidium session he cynically declared: "I thought that I was executing the orders of the Party." In this manner, Stalin's orders concerning the use of methods of physical pressure against the arrested were carried out in practice.

These and many other facts show that all norms of correct Party solution of problems were [in]validated and that everything was dependent upon the willfulness of one man.

The power accumulated in the hands of one person, Stalin, led to serious consequences during the Great Patriotic War.

When we look at many of our novels, films and

historical-scientific studies, the role of Stalin in the Patriotic War appears to be entirely improbable. Stalin had foreseen everything. The Soviet Army, on the basis of a strategic plan prepared by Stalin long before, used the tactics of so-called "active defense," i.e., tactics which, as we know, allowed the Germans to come up to Moscow and Stalingrad. Using such tactics, the Soviet Army, supposedly thanks only to Stalin's genius, turned to the offensive and subdued the enemy. The epic victory gained through the armed might of the land of the Soviets, through our heroic people, is ascribed in this type of novel, film and "scientific study" as being completely due to the strategic genius of Stalin.

We have to analyze this matter carefully because it has a tremendous significance not only from the historical, but especially from the political, educational and practical points of view. What are the facts of this matter?

Before the war, our press and all our political-educational work was characterized by its bragging tone: When an enemy violates the holy Soviet soil, then for every blow of the enemy we will answer with three, and we will battle the enemy on his soil and we will win without much harm to ourselves. But these positive statements were not based in all areas on concrete facts, which would actually guarantee the immunity of our borders.

During the war and after the war, Stalin advanced the thesis that the tragedy our nation experienced in the first part of the war was the result of an "unexpected" attack by the Germans against the Soviet Union. But, comrades, this is completely untrue. As soon as Hitler came to power in Germany he assigned to himself the task of liquidating Communism. The fascists were saying this openly. They did not hide their plans.

In order to attain this aggressive end, all sorts of pacts and blocs were created, such as the famous Berlin-Rome-Tokyo Axis. Many facts from the prewar period clearly showed that Hitler was going all out to begin a war against the Soviet state,

46

and that he had concentrated large armies, together with armored units, near the Soviet borders.

Documents which have now been published show that [as early as] April 3, 1941 Churchill, through his ambassador to the USSR, [Sir Stafford] Cripps, personally warned Stalin that the Germans had begun regrouping their armed units with the intent of attacking the Soviet Union.

It is self-evident that Churchill did not do this at all because of his friendly feeling toward the Soviet nation. He had in this his own imperialistic goals – to bring Germany and the USSR into a bloody war and thereby to strengthen the position of the British Empire.

All the same, Churchill affirmed in his writings that he sought to "warn Stalin and call his attention to the danger which threatened him." Churchill stressed this repeatedly in his dispatches of April 18 and on the following days. However, Stalin took no heed of these warnings. What is more, Stalin ordered that no credence be given to information of this sort, so as not to provoke the initiation of military operations.

We must assert that information of this sort concerning the threat of German armed invasion of Soviet territory was coming in also from our own military and diplomatic sources. However, because the leadership was conditioned against such information, such data was dispatched with fear and assessed with reservation. Thus, for instance, information sent from Berlin on May 6, 1941 by the Soviet military (sic) attaché, Captain (sic) Vorontsov, stated: "Soviet citizen Bozer ... communicated to the Deputy naval attaché that, according to a statement of a certain German officer from Hitler's headquarters, Germany is preparing to invade the USSR on May 14 through Finland, the Baltic countries and Latvia. At the same time Moscow and Leningrad will be heavily raided and paratroopers landed in border cities...."

In his report of May 22, 1941, the Deputy Military

Attaché in Berlin, Khlopov, communicated that "...the attack of the German Army is reportedly scheduled for June 15, but it is possible that it may begin in the first days of June..."

A cable from our London Embassy dated June 18, 1941 stated: "As of now Cripps is deeply convinced of the inevitability of armed conflict between Germany and the USSR, which will begin not later than the middle of June. According to Cripps, the Germans have presently concentrated 147 divisions (including air force and service units) along the Soviet borders...."

Despite these particularly grave warnings, the necessary steps were not taken to prepare the country properly for defense and to prevent it from being caught unawares.

Did we have time and the capabilities for such preparations? Yes, we had the time and the capability. Our industry was already so developed that it was capable of supplying fully the Soviet Army with everything that it needed. This is proven by the fact that, although during the war we lost almost half of our industry and important industrial and food-production areas as the result of enemy occupation of the Ukraine, Northern Caucasus and other western parts of the country, the Soviet nation was still able to organize the production of military equipment in the eastern parts of the country, to install there equipment taken from the western industrial areas, and to supply our armed forces with everything necessary to destroy the enemy.

Had our industry been mobilized properly and in time to supply the Army with the necessary materiel, our wartime losses would have been decidedly smaller. However such mobilization had not been started in time. And already in the first days of the war it became evident that our Army was badly armed. We did not have enough artillery, tanks and planes to throw the enemy back.

Soviet science and technology produced excellent

models of tanks and artillery pieces before the war. But mass production of all this was not organized. As a matter of fact, we started to modernize our military equipment only on the eve of the war. As a result, when the enemy invaded Soviet territory we did not have sufficient quantities either of old machinery which was no longer used for armament production or of new machinery which we had planned to introduce into armament production.

The situation with anti-aircraft artillery was especially bad. We did not organize the production of anti-tank ammunition. Many fortified regions proved to be indefensible as soon as they were attacked, because their old arms had been withdrawn and new ones were not yet available there.

This pertained, alas, not only to tanks, artillery and planes. At the outbreak of the war we did not even have sufficient numbers of rifles to arm the mobilized manpower. I recall that in those days I telephoned from Kiev to comrade [Georgy] Malenkov and told him, "People have volunteered for the new Army [units] and are demanding weapons. You must send us arms."

Malenkov answered me, "We cannot send you arms. We are sending all our rifles to Leningrad and you have to arm yourselves."

(Movement in the hall.)

Such was the armament situation.

In this connection we cannot forget, for instance, the following fact: Shortly before the invasion of the Soviet Union by Hitler's army, [Colonel-General M. P.] Kirponos, who was chief of the Kiev Special Military District (he was later killed at the front), wrote to Stalin that German armies were at the Bug River, were preparing for an attack and in the very near future would probably start their offensive. In this connection, Kirponos proposed that a strong defense be organized, that 300,000 people be evacuated from the border areas and that several strong points be organized there: anti-tank ditches, trenches for the soldiers, etc.

Moscow answered this proposition with the assertions that this would be a provocation, that no preparatory defensive work should be undertaken at the borders, and that the Germans were not to be given any pretext for the initiation of military action against us. Thus our borders were insufficiently prepared to repel the enemy.

When the fascist armies had actually invaded Soviet territory and military operations began, Moscow issued an order that German fire was not to be returned. Why? It was because Stalin, despite the self-evident facts, thought that the war had not yet started, that this was only a provocative action on the part of several undisciplined sections of the German Army, and that our reaction might serve as a reason for the Germans to begin the war.

The following fact is also known: On the eve of the invasion of Soviet territory by Hitler's army, a certain German citizen crossed our border and stated that the German armies had received orders to start [their] offensive against the Soviet Union on the night of June 22 at 3 o'clock. Stalin was informed about this immediately, but even this warning was ignored.

As you see, everything was ignored: warnings of certain Army commanders, declarations of deserters from the enemy army, and even the open hostility of the enemy. Is this an example of the alertness of the chief of the Party and of the state at this particularly significant historical moment?

And what were the results of this carefree attitude, this disregard of clear facts? The result was that already in the first hours and days the enemy had destroyed in our border regions a large part of our Air Force, our artillery and other military equipment. [Stalin] annihilated large numbers of our military cadres and disorganized our military leadership. Consequently we could not prevent the enemy from marching deep into the country.

Very grievous consequences, especially with regard to the beginning of the war, followed Stalin's annihilation of many military commanders and political workers during 1937-1941 because of his suspiciousness and through slanderous accusations. During these years repressions were instituted against certain parts of our military cadres beginning literally at the company- and battalion-commander levels and extending to higher military centers. During this time, the cadre of leaders who had gained military experience in Spain and in the Far East was almost completely liquidated.

The policy of large-scale repression against military cadres led also to undermined military discipline, because for several years officers of all ranks and even soldiers in Party and Komsomol cells were taught to "unmask" their superiors as hidden enemies.

(Movement in the hall.)

It is natural that this caused a negative influence on the state of military discipline in the initial stage of the war.

And, as you know, we had before the war excellent military cadres which were unquestionably loyal to the Party and to the Fatherland. Suffice it to say that those of them who managed to survive, despite severe tortures to which they were subjected in the prisons, have from the first war days shown themselves real patriots and heroically fought for the glory of the Fatherland. I have here in mind such [generals] as: [Konstantin] Rokossovsky (who, as you know, had been jailed); [Alexander] Gorbatov; [Kiril] Meretskov (who is a delegate at the present Congress); [K. P.] Podlas (he was an excellent commander who perished at the front); and many, many others. However, many such commanders perished in the camps and the jails and the Army saw them no more.

All this brought about a situation at the beginning of the war that was a great threat to our Fatherland.

51

It would be wrong to forget that, after [our] severe initial disaster[s] and defeat[s] at the front, Stalin thought that it was the end. In one of his [declarations] in those days he said: "Lenin left us a great legacy and we've lost it forever."

After this Stalin for a long time actually did not direct military operations and ceased to do anything whatsoever. He returned to active leadership only when a Politbiuro delegation visited him and told him that steps needed to be taken immediately so as to improve the situation at the front.

Therefore, the threatening danger which hung over our Fatherland in the initial period of the war was largely due to Stalin's very own faulty methods of directing the nation and the Party.

However, we speak not only about the moment when the war began, which led to our Army's serious disorganization and brought us severe losses. Even after the war began, the nervousness and hysteria which Stalin demonstrated while interfering with actual military operations caused our Army serious damage.

Stalin was very far from understanding the real situation that was developing at the front. This was natural because, during the whole Patriotic War, he never visited any section of the front or any liberated city except for one short ride on the Mozhaisk highway during a stabilized situation at the front. To this incident were dedicated many literary works full of fantasies of all sorts and so many paintings. Simultaneously, Stalin was interfering with operations and issuing orders which did not take into consideration the real situation at a given section of the front and which could not help but result in huge personnel losses.

I will allow myself in this connection to bring out one characteristic fact which illustrates how Stalin directed operations at the fronts. Present at this Congress is Marshal [Ivan] Bagramyan, who was once the head of operations in the

Southwestern Front Headquarters and who can corroborate what I will tell you.

When an exceptionally serious situation for our Army developed in the Kharkov region in 1942, we correctly decided to drop an operation whose objective was to encircle [the city]. The real situation at that time would have threatened our Army with fatal consequences if this operation were continued.

We communicated this to Stalin, stating that the situation demanded changes in [our] operational plans so that the enemy would be prevented from liquidating a sizable concentration of our Army.

Contrary to common sense, Stalin rejected our suggestion. He issued the order to continue the encirclement of Kharkov, despite the fact that at this time many [of our own] Army concentrations actually were threatened with encirclement and liquidation.

I telephoned to [Marshal Alexander] Vasilevsky and begged him: "Alexander Mikhailovich, take a map" – Vasilevsky is present here – "and show comrade Stalin the situation that has developed." We should note that Stalin planned operations on a globe.

(Animation in the hall.)

Yes, comrades, he used to take a globe and trace the front line on it. I said to comrade Vasilevsky: "Show him the situation on a map. In the present situation we cannot continue the operation which was planned. The old decision must be changed for the good of the cause."

Vasilevsky replied, saying that Stalin had already studied this problem. He said that he, Vasilevsky, would not see Stalin further concerning this matter, because the latter didn't want to hear any arguments on the subject of this operation.

After my talk with Vasilevsky, I telephoned to Stalin at his *dacha*. But Stalin did not answer the phone and Malenkov was at the receiver. I told comrade Malenkov that I was calling from the front and that I wanted to speak personally to Stalin. Stalin informed me through Malenkov that I should speak with Malenkov. I stated for the second time that I wished to inform Stalin personally about the grave situation which had arisen for us at the front. But Stalin did not consider it convenient to pick up the phone and again stated that I should speak to him through Malenkov, although he was only a few steps from the telephone.

After "listening" in this manner to our plea, Stalin said: "Let everything remain as it is!"

And what was the result of this? The worst we had expected. The Germans surrounded our Army concentrations and as a result [the Kharkov counterattack] lost hundreds of thousands of our soldiers. This is Stalin's military "genius." This is what it cost us.

(Movement in the hall.)

On one occasion after the war, during a meeting [between] Stalin [and] members of the Politbiuro, Anastas Ivanovich Mikoyan mentioned that Khrushchev must have been right when he telephoned concerning the Kharkov operation and that it was unfortunate that his suggestion had not been accepted.

You should have seen Stalin's fury! How could it be admitted that he, Stalin, had not been right! He is after all a "genius," and a genius cannot help but be right! Everyone can err, but Stalin considered that he never erred, that he was always right. He never acknowledged to anyone that he made any mistake, large or small, despite the fact that he made more than a few in matters of theory and in his practical activity. After the Party Congress we shall probably have to re-evaluate many [of our] wartime military operations and present them in their true light.

The tactics on which Stalin insisted – without knowing

the basics of conducting battle operations – cost much blood until we succeeded in stopping the opponent and going over to the offensive.

The military knows that as late as the end of 1941, instead of great operational maneuvers flanking [our] opponent and penetrating behind his back, Stalin was demanding incessant frontal [counter-]attacks and the [re-]capture of one village after another.

Because of this, we paid with great losses – until our generals, upon whose shoulders the whole weight of conducting the war rested, succeeded in altering the situation and shifting to flexible-maneuver operations. [This] immediately brought serious changes at the front [that were] favorable to us.

All the more shameful was the fact that after our great victory over the enemy, which cost us so dearly, Stalin began to downgrade many of the commanders who had contributed so much to it. [This was] because Stalin ruled out any chance that services rendered at the front might be credited to anyone but himself.

Stalin was very much interested in assessments of comrade [Grigory] Zhukov as a military leader. He asked me often for my opinion of Zhukov. I told him then, "I have known Zhukov for a long time. He is a good general and a good military leader."

After the war Stalin began to tell all kinds of nonsense about Zhukov. Among it [was] the following: "You praised Zhukov, but he does not deserve it. They say that before each operation at the front Zhukov used to behave as follows: He used to take a handful of earth, smell it and say, 'We can begin the attack,' or its opposite, 'The planned operation cannot be carried out.'" I stated at the time, "Comrade Stalin, I do not know who invented this, but it is not true."

It is possible that Stalin himself invented these things for the purpose of minimizing the role and military talents of

Marshal Zhukov.

In this connection, Stalin very energetically popularized himself as a great leader. In various ways he tried to inculcate the notion that the victories gained by the Soviet nation during the Great Patriotic War were all due to the courage, daring, and genius of Stalin and of no one else. Just like [a] Kuzma Kryuchkov, he put one dress on seven people at the same time.

(Animation in the hall.)

In the same vein, let us take for instance our historical and military films and some [of our] literary creations. They make us feel sick. Their true objective is propagating the theme of praising Stalin as a military genius. Let us recall the film, *The Fall of Berlin*. Here only Stalin acts. He issues orders in a hall in which there are many empty Chairs. Only only one man approaches him to report something to him – it is [Alexander] Poskrebyshev, his loyal shield-bearer.

(Laughter in the hall.)

And where is the military command? Where is the Politburo? Where is the Government? What are they doing, and with what are they engaged? There is nothing about them in the film. Stalin acts for everybody, he does not reckon with anyone. He asks no one for advice. Everything is shown to the people in this false light. Why? To surround Stalin with glory– contrary to the facts and contrary to historical truth.

The question arises: Where is the military, on whose shoulders rested the burden of the war? It is not in the film. With Stalin's inclusion, there was no room left for it.

Not Stalin, but the Party as a whole, the Soviet Government, our heroic Army, its talented leaders and brave soldiers, the whole Soviet nation – these are the ones who assured victory in the Great Patriotic War.

(Tempestuous and prolonged applause.)

Central Committee members, Ministers, our economic

leaders, the leaders of Soviet culture, directors of territorial-party and Soviet organizations, engineers, and technicians – every one of them in his own place of work generously gave of his strength and knowledge toward ensuring victory over the enemy.

Exceptional heroism was shown by our hard core – surrounded by glory are our whole working class, our kolkhoz peasantry, the Soviet intelligentsia, who under the leadership of Party organizations overcame untold hardships and bearing the hardships of war, and devoted all their strength to the cause of the Fatherland's defense.

Our Soviet women accomplished great and brave deeds during the war. They bore on their backs the heavy load of production work in the factories, on the kolkhozes, and in various economic and cultural sectors. Many women participated directly in the Great Patriotic War at the front. Our brave youth contributed immeasurably, both at the front and at home, to the defense of the Soviet Fatherland and to the annihilation of the enemy.

The services of Soviet soldiers, of our commanders and political workers of all ranks are immortal. After the loss of a considerable part of the Army in the initial war months, they did not lose their heads and were able to reorganize during the course of combat. Over the course of the war they created and toughened a strong, heroic Army. They not only withstood [our] strong and cunning enemy's pressure but smashed him.

The magnificent, heroic deeds of hundreds of millions of people of the East and of the West during the fight against the threat of fascist subjugation which loomed before us will live for centuries, [indeed] for millennia in the memory of thankful humanity.

(Thunderous applause.)

The main roles and the main credit for the victorious ending of the war belong to our Communist Party, to the armed forces of the Soviet Union, and to the tens of millions of Soviet people uplifted by the Party.

(Thunderous and prolonged applause.)

Comrades, let us reach for some other facts. The Soviet Union justly is considered a model multinational state because we have assured in practice the equality and friendship of all [of the] peoples living in our great Fatherland.

All the more monstrous are those acts whose initiator was Stalin and which were rude violations of the basic Leninist principles [behind our] Soviet state's nationalities policies. We refer to the mass deportations of entire nations from their places of origin, together with all Communists and Komsomols without any exception. This deportation was not dictated by any military considerations.

Thus, at the end of 1943, when there already had been a permanent change of fortune at the front in favor of the Soviet Union, a decision concerning the deportation of all the Karachai from the lands on which they lived was taken and executed.

In the same period, at the end of December, 1943, the same lot befell the [Kalmyks] of the Kalmyk Autonomous Republic. In March, 1944, all the Chechens and Ingushi were deported and the Chechen-Ingush Autonomous Republic was liquidated. In April, 1944, all Balkars were deported from the territory of the Kabardino-Balkar Autonomous Republic to faraway places and their Republic itself was renamed the Autonomous Kabardian Republic.

Ukrainians avoided meeting this fate only because there were too many of them and there was no place to which to deport them. Otherwise, [Stalin] would have deported them also.

(Laughter and animation in the hall.)

No Marxist-Leninist, no man of common sense can grasp how it is possible to make whole nations responsible for inimical activity, including women, children, old people, Communists and Komsomols, to use mass repression against them, and to expose them to misery and suffering for the hostile acts of individual persons or groups of persons.

After the conclusion of the Patriotic War, the Soviet nation proudly stressed the magnificent victories gained through [our] great sacrifices and tremendous efforts. The country experienced a period of political enthusiasm. The Party came out of the war even more united. Its cadres were tempered and hardened by the fire of the war. Under such conditions nobody could have even thought of the possibility of some plot in the Party.

And it was precisely at this time that the so-called "Leningrad affair" was born. As we have now proven, this case was fabricated. Those who innocently lost their lives included: comrades [Nikolay] Voznesensky, [Aleksey] Kuznetsov, [Mikhail] Rodionov, [Pyotr] Popkov, and others.

As is known, Voznesensky and Kuznetsov were talented and eminent leaders. Once they stood very close to Stalin. It is sufficient to mention that Stalin made Voznesensky First Deputy to the Chairman of the Council of Ministers and Kuznetsov was elected Secretary of the Central Committee. The very fact that Stalin entrusted Kuznetsov with the supervision of the state-security organs shows the trust which he enjoyed.

How did it happen that these persons were branded as enemies of the people and liquidated?

Facts prove that the "Leningrad affair" is also the result of willfulness which Stalin exercised against Party cadres. Had a normal situation existed in the Party's Central Committee and in the Central Committee Politbiuro, affairs of this nature would have been examined there in accordance with Party practice, and all pertinent facts assessed; as a result, such an affair as well as others would not have happened.

We must state that, after the war, the situation became

even more complicated. Stalin became even more capricious, irritable and brutal. In particular, his suspicion grew. His persecution mania reached unbelievable dimensions. Many workers became enemies before his very eyes. After the war, Stalin separated himself from the collective even more. Everything was decided by him alone without any consideration for anyone or anything.

This unbelievable suspicion was cleverly taken advantage of by the abject provocateur and vile enemy, Beria, who murdered thousands of Communists and loyal Soviet people. The elevation of Voznesensky and Kuznetsov alarmed Beria. As we have now proven, it had been precisely Beria who had "suggested" to Stalin the fabrication by him and by his confidants of materials in the form of declarations and anonymous letters, and in the form of various rumors and talks.

The Party's Central Committee has examined this so-called "Leningrad affair"; persons who innocently suffered are now rehabilitated and honor has been restored to the glorious Leningrad Party organization. [V. S.] Abakumov and others who had fabricated this affair were brought before a court; their trial took place in Leningrad and they received what they deserved.

The question arises: Why is it that we see the truth of this affair only now, and why did we not do something earlier, during Stalin's life, in order to prevent the loss of innocent lives? It was because Stalin personally supervised the "Leningrad affair," and the majority of the Politbiuro members did not, at that time, know all of the circumstances in these matters and could not therefore intervene.

When Stalin received certain material from Beria and Abakumov, without examining these slanderous materials he ordered an investigation of the "affair" of Voznesensky and Kuznetsov. With this, their fate was sealed.

Similarly instructive is the case of the Mingrelian nationalist organization which supposedly existed in Georgia.

As is known, resolutions by the Central Committee, Communist Party of the Soviet Union, were made concerning this case in November 1951 and in March 1952. These resolutions were made without prior discussion with the Politbiuro. Stalin had personally dictated them. They made serious accusations against many loyal Communists. On the basis of falsified documents, it was proven that there existed in Georgia a supposedly nationalistic organization whose objective was the liquidation of the Soviet power in that republic with the help of imperialist powers.

In this connection, a number of responsible Party and Soviet workers were arrested in Georgia. As was later proven, this was a slander directed against the Georgian Party organization.

We know that there have been at times manifestations of local bourgeois nationalism in Georgia as in several other republics. The question arises: Could it be possible that, in the period during which the resolutions referred to above were made, nationalist tendencies grew so much that there was a danger of Georgia's leaving the Soviet Union and joining Turkey?

(Animation in the hall, laughter).

This is, of course, nonsense. It is impossible to imagine how such assumptions could enter anyone's mind. Everyone knows how Georgia has developed economically and culturally under Soviet rule. Industrial production in the Georgian Republic is 27 times greater than it was before the Revolution. Many new industries have arisen in Georgia which did not exist there before the Revolution: iron smelting, an oil industry, a machine-construction industry, etc. Illiteracy has long since been liquidated, which, in pre-Revolutionary Georgia, included 78 per cent of the population.

Could the Georgians, comparing the situation in their republic with the hard situation of the working masses in

Turkey, be aspiring to join Turkey? In 1955, Georgia produced 18 times as much steel per person as Turkey. Georgia produces 9 times as much electrical energy per person as Turkey. According to the available 1950 census, 65 per cent of Turkey's total population is illiterate, and 80 per cent of its women. Georgia has 19 institutions of higher learning which have about 39,000 students; this is 8 times more than in Turkey (for each 1,000 inhabitants). The prosperity of the working people has grown tremendously in Georgia under Soviet rule.

It is clear that, as the economy and culture develop, and as the socialist consciousness of the working masses in Georgia grows, the source from which bourgeois nationalism draws its strength evaporates.

As it developed, there was no nationalistic organization in Georgia. Thousands of innocent people fell victim to willfulness and lawlessness. All of this happened under the "genius" leadership of Stalin, "the great son of the Georgian nation," as Georgians like to refer to him.

(Animation in the hall.)

The willfulness of Stalin showed itself not only in decisions concerning the internal life of the country but also in the international relations of the Soviet Union.

The July Plenum of the Central Committee studied in detail the reasons for the development of conflict with Yugoslavia. It was a shameful role which Stalin played here. The "Yugoslav affair" contained no problems which could not have been solved through Party discussions among comrades. There was no significant basis for the development of this "affair." It was completely possible to have prevented the rupture of relations with that country. This does not mean, however, that Yugoslav leaders made no mistakes or had no shortcomings. But these mistakes and shortcomings were magnified in a monstrous manner by Stalin, resulting in the breakoff of relations with a friendly country.

I recall the first days when the conflict between the Soviet Union and Yugoslavia began to be blown up artificially. Once, when I came from Kiev to Moscow, I was invited to visit Stalin, who, pointing to the copy of a letter recently sent to [Yugoslavian President Marshal Joseph] Tito, asked me, "Have you read this?"

Not waiting for my reply, he answered, "I will shake my little finger – and there will be no more Tito. He will fall."

We have paid dearly for this "shaking of the little finger." This statement reflected Stalin's mania for greatness, but he acted just that way: "I will shake my little finger – and there will be no Kosior"; "I will shake my little finger once more and Postyshev and Chubar will be no more"; "I will shake my little finger again – and Voznesensky, Kuznetsov and many others will disappear."

But this did not happen to Tito. No matter how much or how little Stalin shook, not only his little finger but everything else that he could shake, Tito did not fall. Why? The reason was that, in this instance of disagreement with [our] Yugoslav comrades, Tito had behind him a state and a people who had had a serious education in fighting for liberty and independence, a people who gave support to its leaders.

You see what Stalin's mania for greatness led to. He completely lost consciousness of reality. He demonstrated his suspicion and haughtiness not only in relation to individuals in the USSR, but in relation to whole parties and nations.

We have carefully examined the case of Yugoslavia. We have found a proper solution which is approved by the peoples of the Soviet Union and of Yugoslavia as well as by the working masses of all the people's democracies and by all progressive humanity. The liquidation of [our] abnormal relationship with Yugoslavia was done in the interest of the whole camp of socialism, in the interest of strengthening peace in the whole world.

Let us also recall the "affair of the doctor-plotters."

(Animation in the hall.)

Actually there was no "affair" outside of the declaration of the woman doctor [Lidiya] Timashuk, who was probably influenced or ordered by someone (after all, she was an unofficial collaborator of the organs of state security) to write Stalin a letter in which she declared that doctors were applying supposedly improper methods of medical treatment.

Such a letter was sufficient for Stalin to reach an immediate conclusion that there are doctor-plotters in the Soviet Union. He issued orders to arrest a group of eminent Soviet medical specialists. He personally issued advice on the conduct of the investigation and the method of interrogation of the arrested persons. He said that academician [V. N.] Vinogradov should be put in chains, and that another one [of the alleged plotters] should be beaten. The former Minister of State Security, comrade [Semyen] Ignatiev, is present at this Congress as a delegate. Stalin told him curtly, "If you do not obtain confessions from the doctors we will shorten you by a head."

(Tumult in the hall.)

Stalin personally called the investigative judge, gave him instructions, and advised him on which investigative methods should be used. These methods were simple – beat, beat and, beat again.

Shortly after the doctors were arrested, we members of the Politbiuro received protocols with the doctors' confessions of guilt. After distributing these protocols, Stalin told us, "You are blind like young kittens. What will happen without me? The country will perish because you do not know how to recognize enemies."

The case was presented so that no one could verify the facts on which the investigation was based. There was no possibility of trying to verify facts by contacting those who had made the confessions of guilt.

We felt, however, that the case of the arrested doctors was questionable. We knew some of these people personally because they had once treated us. When we examined this "case" after Stalin's death, we found it to have been fabricated from beginning to end.

This ignominious "case" was set up by Stalin. He did not, however, have the time in which to bring it to an end (as he conceived that end), and for this reason the doctors are still alive. All of them have been rehabilitated. They are working in the same places they were working before. They are treating top individuals, not excluding members of the Government. They have our full confidence; and they execute their duties honestly, as they did before.

In putting together various dirty and shameful cases, a very base role was played by a rabid enemy of our Party, an agent of a foreign intelligence service – Beria, who had stolen into Stalin's confidence. How could this provocateur have gained such a position in the Party and in the state, so as to become the First Deputy Chair of the Council of Ministers of the Soviet Union and a Politbiuro member? It has now been established that this villain climbed up the Government ladder over an untold number of corpses.

Were there any signs that Beria was an enemy of the Party? Yes, there were. Already in 1937, at a Central Committee Plenum, former People's Commissar of Health [Grigory] Kaminsky said that Beria worked for the Musavat intelligence service. But the Plenum had barely concluded when Kaminsky was arrested and then shot. Had Stalin examined Kaminsky's statement? No, because Stalin believed in Beria, and that was enough for him. And when Stalin believed in anyone or anything, then no one could say anything that was contrary to his opinion. Anyone daring to express opposition would have met the same fate as Kaminsky.

There were other signs, also. The declaration which comrade [A. V.] Snegov made to the Party's Central Committee isinteresting. (Parenthetically speaking, he was also rehabilitated not long ago, after 17 years in prison camps.) In this declaration, Snegov writes:

"In connection with the proposed rehabilitation of the former Central Committee member, [Lavrenty] Kartvelishvili-Lavrentiev, I have entrusted to the hands of the representative of the Committee of State Security a detailed deposition concerning Beria's role in the disposition of the Kartvelishvili case and concerning the criminal motives by which Beria was guided.

"In my opinion, it is indispensable to recall an important fact pertaining to this case and to communicate it to the Central Committee, because I did not consider it as proper to include in the investigation documents.

"On October 30, 1931, at a session of the Organizational Bureau of the Central Committee of the All-Union Communist Party (Bolsheviks), Kartvelishvili, Secretary of the Transcaucasian Regional Committee, made a report. All members of the executive of the Regional Committee were present. Of them I alone am now alive.

"During this session, J. V. Stalin made a motion at the end of his speech concerning the organization of the secretariat of the Transcaucasian Regional Committee composed of the following: First Secretary, Kartvelishvili; Second Secretary, Beria (it was then, for the first time in the Party's history, that Beria's name was mentioned as a candidate for a Party position). Kartvelishvili answered that he knew Beria well and for that reason refused categorically to work together with him. Stalin proposed then that this matter be left open and that it be solved in the process of the work itself. Two days later a decision was arrived at that Beria would receive the Party post and that Kartvelishvili would be deported from the Transcaucasus.

"This fact can be confirmed by comrades Mikoyan and

Kaganovich, who were present at that session."

The long, unfriendly relations between Kartvelishvili and Beria were widely known. They date back to the time when comrade Sergo [Ordzhonikidze] was active in the Transcaucasus. Kartvelishvili was the closest assistant of Sergo. The unfriendly relationship impelled Beria to fabricate a "case" against Kartvelishvili. It is characteristic that Kartvelishvili was charged with a terroristic act against Beria in this "case."

The indictment in the Beria case contains a discussion of his crimes. Some things should, however, be recalled, especially since it is possible that not all delegates to the Congress have read this document. I wish to recall Beria's bestial disposition of the cases of [Mikhail] Kedrov, [V.] Golubev, and Golubev's adopted mother, Baturina – persons who wished to inform the Central Committee concerning Beria's treacherous activity. They were shot without any trial and the sentence was passed ex post facto, after the execution.

Here is what the old Communist, comrade Kedrov, wrote to the Central Committee through comrade [Andrey] Andreyev (comrade Andreyev was then a Central Committee Secretary):

"I am calling to you for help from a gloomy cell of the Lefortovo prison. Let my cry of horror reach your ears; do not remain deaf, take me under your protection; please, help remove the nightmare of interrogations and show that this is all a mistake.

"I suffer innocently. Please believe me. Time will testify to the truth. I am not an agent provocateur of the Tsarist Okhrana. I am not a spy, I am not a member of an anti-Soviet organization of which I am being accused on the basis of denunciations. I am also not guilty of any other crimes against the Party and the Government. I am an old Bolshevik, free of any stain; I have honestly fought for almost 40 years in the ranks of the Party for the good and prosperity of the nation....

"... Today I, a 62-year-old man, am being threatened by the investigative judges with more severe, cruel and degrading methods of physical pressure. They (the judges) are no longer capable of becoming aware of their error and of recognizing that their handling of my case is illegal and impermissible. They try to justify their actions by picturing me as a hardened and raving enemy and are demanding increased repressions. But let the Party know that I am innocent and that there is nothing which can turn a loyal son of the Party into an enemy, even right up to his last dying breath.

"But I have no way out. I cannot divert from myself the hastily approaching new and powerful blows.

"Everything, however, has its limits. My torture has reached the extreme. My health is broken, my strength and my energy are waning, the end is drawing near. To die in a Soviet prison, branded as a vile traitor to the Fatherland – what can be more monstrous for an honest man? And how monstrous all this is! Unsurpassed bitterness and pain grips my heart. No! No! This will not happen; this cannot be, I cry. Neither the Party, nor the Soviet Government, nor the People's Commissar, L. P. Beria, will permit this cruel, ireparable injustice. I am firmly certain that, given a quiet, objective examination, without any foul rantings, without any anger and without the fearful tortures, it would be easy to prove the baselessness of the charges. I believe deeply that truth and justice will triumph. I believe. I believe."

The old Bolshevik, comrade Kedrov, was found innocent by the Military Collegium. But, despite this, he was shot at Beria's order.

(Indignation in the hall.)

Beria also handled cruelly the family of comrade Ordzhonikidze. Why? Because Ordzhonikidze had tried to prevent Beria from realizing his shameful plans. Beria had cleared from his way all persons who could possibly interfere with him. Ordzhonikidze was always an opponent of Beria, which he told to Stalin. Instead of examining this affair and taking appropriate steps, Stalin allowed the liquidation of Ordzhonikidze's brother and brought Ordzhonikidze himself to such a state that he was forced to shoot himself.

(Indignation in the hall.)

Beria was unmasked by the Party's Central Committee shortly after Stalin's death. As a result of particularly detailed legal proceedings, it was established that Beria had committed monstrous crimes and Beria was shot.

The question arises why Beria, who had liquidated tens of thousands of Party and Soviet workers, was not unmasked during Stalin's life. He was not unmasked earlier because he had utilized very skillfully Stalin's weaknesses; feeding him with suspicions, he assisted Stalin in everything and acted with his support.

Comrades: The cult of the individual acquired such monstrous size chiefly because Stalin himself, using all conceivable methods, supported the glorification of his own person. This is supported by numerous facts. One of the most characteristic examples of Stalin's self-glorification and of his lack of even elementary modesty is the edition of his *Short Biography*, which was published in 1948 (sic).

This book is an expression of the most dissolute flattery, an example of making a man into a godhead, of transforming him into an infallible sage, "the greatest leader, sublime strategist of all times and nations." Finally, no other words could be found with which to lift Stalin up to the heavens.

We need not give here examples of the loathesome adulation filling this book. All we need to add is that they all were approved and edited by Stalin personally. Some of them were added in his own handwriting to the draft text of the book.

What did Stalin consider essential to write into this book? Did he want to cool the ardor of the flatterers who were composing his *Short Biography*? No! He marked the very places where he thought that the praise of his services was insufficient. Here are some examples characterizing Stalin's activity, added in Stalin's own hand:

"In this fight against the skeptics and capitulators, the Trotskyites, Zinovievites, Bukharinites and Kamenevites, there was definitely welded together, after Lenin's death, that leading core of the Party... that upheld the great banner of Lenin, rallied the Party behind Lenin's behests, and brought the Soviet people onto the broad paths of industrializing the country and collectivizing the rural economy. The leader of this core and the guiding force of the Party and the state was comrade Stalin."

Thus writes Stalin himself! Then he adds:

"Although he performed his tasks as leader of the Party and the people with consummate skill, and enjoyed the unreserved support of the entire Soviet people, Stalin never allowed his work to be marred by the slightest hint of vanity, conceit or self-adulation."

Where and when could a leader so praise himself? Is this worthy of a leader of the Marxist-Leninist type? No. Precisely against this did Marx and Engels take such a strong position. This always was sharply condemned also by Vladimir Ilyich Lenin.

In the draft text of [Stalin's] book appeared the following sentence: "Stalin is the Lenin of today." This sentence appeared to Stalin to be too weak. Thus, in his own handwriting, he changed it to read: "Stalin is the worthy continuer of Lenin's work, or, as it is said in our Party, Stalin is the Lenin of today." You see how well it is said, not by the nation but by Stalin himself.

It is possible to offer many such self-praising appraisals written into the draft text of that book in Stalin's hand. He showers himself especially generously with praises regarding his military genius and his talent for strategy. I will cite one more insertion made by Stalin on the theme: "The advanced Soviet science of war received further development," he writes, "at Comrade Stalin's hands. Comrade Stalin elaborated the theory of the permanent operating factors that decide the issue of wars, of active defense and the laws of counteroffensive and offensive, of the cooperation of all services and arms in modern warfare, of the role of big tank masses and air forces in modern war, and of the artillery as the most formidable of the armed services. At various stages of the war, Stalin's genius found correct solutions that took into account all the circumstances of the situation."

(Movement in the hall.)

Further, Stalin writes: "Stalin's military mastership was displayed both in defense and on offense. Comrade Stalin's genius enabled him to divine the enemy's plans and defeat them. The battles in which comrade Stalin directed the Soviet armies are brilliant examples of operational military skill."

This is how Stalin was praised as a strategist. Who did this? Stalin himself, not in his role as a strategist but in the role of an author-editor, one of the main creators of his [own] self-adulatory biography. Such, comrades, are the facts. Or should be said, rather, the shameful facts.

One additional fact from the same *Short Biography* of Stalin: As is known, the *History of the All-Union Communist Party (Bolsheviks), Short Course* was written by a commission of the Party Central Committee.

This book, parenthetically, was also permeated with the cult of the individual and was written by a designated group of authors. This fact was reflected in the following formulation on the proof copy of the *Short Biography* of Stalin: "A commission of the Central Committee, All-Union Communist Party (Bolsheviks), under the direction of comrade Stalin and with his most active personal participation, has prepared a *History of the All-Union Communist Party (Bolsheviks), Short Course*."

But even this phrase did not satisfy Stalin: The following sentence replaced it in the final version of the *Short Biography*: "In 1938, the book *History of the All-Union Communist Party (Bolsheviks), Short Course* appeared, written by comrade Stalin and approved by a commission of the Central Committee, All-Union Communist Party (Bolsheviks)." Can one add anything more?

(Animation in the hall.)

As you see, a surprising metamorphosis changed the work created by a group into a book written by Stalin. It is not necessary to state how and why this metamorphosis took place.

A pertinent question comes to our mind: If Stalin is the author of this book, why did he need to praise the person of Stalin so much and to transform the whole post-October historical period of our glorious Communist Party solely into an action of "the Stalin genius"?

Did this book properly reflect the efforts of the Party in the socialist transformation of the country, in the construction of socialist society, in the industrialization and collectivization of the country, and also other steps taken by the Party which undeviatingly traveled the path outlined by Lenin? This book speaks principally about Stalin, about his speeches, about his reports. Everything without the smallest exception is tied to his name.

And when Stalin himself asserts that he himself wrote the *Short Course,* this calls at least for amazement. Can a Marxist-Leninist thus write about himself, praising his own person to the heavens?

Or let us take the matter of the Stalin Prizes.

(Movement in the hall.)

Not even the Tsars created prizes which they named after themselves.

Stalin recognized as the best a text of the national

anthem of the Soviet Union which contains not a word about the Communist Party; it contains, however, the following unprecedented praise of Stalin: "Stalin brought us up in loyalty to the people. He inspired us to great toil and deeds."

In these lines of the anthem, the whole educational, directional and inspirational activity of the great Leninist Party is ascribed to Stalin. This is, of course, a clear deviation from Marxism-Leninism, a clear debasing and belittling of the role of the Party. We should add for your information that the Presidium of the Central Committee has already passed a resolution concerning the composition of a new text of the anthem. which will reflect the role of the people and the role of the Party.

(Loud, prolonged applause.)

And was it without Stalin's knowledge that many of the largest enterprises and towns were named after him? Was it without his knowledge that Stalin monuments were erected in the whole country – these "memorials to the living"? It is a fact that Stalin himself had signed on July 2, 1951 a resolution of the USSR Council of Ministers concerning the erection on the Volga-Don Canal of an impressive monument to Stalin; on September 4 of the same year he issued an order making 33 tons of copper available for the construction of this impressive monument.

Anyone who has visited the Stalingrad area must have seen the huge statue which is being built there, and that on a site which hardly any people frequent. Huge sums were spent to build it at a time when people of this area had lived since the war in huts. Consider, yourself, was Stalin right when he wrote in his biography that "...he did not allow in himself... even a shadow of conceit, pride, or self-adoration"?

At the same time Stalin gave proofs of his lack of respect for Lenin's memory. It is not a coincidence that, despite the decision taken over 30 years ago to build a Palace of Soviets as a monument to Vladimir Ilyich, this palace was not built, its construction was always postponed and the project allowed to lapse.

We cannot forget to recall the Soviet Government resolution of August 14, 1925 concerning "the founding of Lenin prizes for educational work." This resolution was published in the press, but until this day there are no Lenin prizes. This, too, should be corrected.

(Tumultuous, prolonged applause.)

During Stalin's life – thanks to known methods which I have mentioned, and quoting facts, for instance. from the *Short Biography* of Stalin – all events were explained as if Lenin played only a secondary role, even during the October Socialist Revolution. In many films and in many literary works the figure of Lenin was incorrectly presented and inadmissibly depreciated.

Stalin loved to see the film *The Unforgettable Year of 1919*, in which he was shown on the steps of an armored train and where he was practically vanquishing the foe with his own saber. Let Klimenty Yefremovich [Voroshilov], our dear friend, find the necessary courage and write the truth about Stalin; after all, he knows how Stalin had fought. It will be difficult for comrade Voroshilov to undertake this, but it would be good if he did it. Everyone will approve of it, both the people and the Party. Even his grandsons will thank him.

(Prolonged applause.)

In speaking about the events of the October Revolution and about the Civil War, the impression was created that Stalin always played the main role, as if everywhere and always Stalin had suggested to Lenin what to do and how to do it. However, this is slander of Lenin.

(Prolonged applause.)

I will probably not sin against the truth when I say that

74

99 per cent of the persons present here heard and knew very little about Stalin before the year 1924, while Lenin was known to all. He was known to the whole Party, to the whole nation, from children all the way up to old men.

(Tumultuous, prolonged applause.)

All this has to be thoroughly revised so that history, literature and the fine arts properly reflect V. I. Lenin's role and the great deeds of our Communist Party and of the Soviet people – a creative people.

(Applause.)

Comrades! The cult of the individual caused the employment of faulty principles in Party work and in economic activity. It brought about rude violation of internal Party and Soviet democracy, sterile administration, deviations of all sorts, cover-ups of shortcomings, and varnishings of reality. Our nation bore forth many flatterers and specialists in false optimism and deceit.

We should also not forget that, due to the numerous arrests of Party, Soviet and economic leaders, many workers began to work uncertainly, showed overcautiousness, feared all which was new, feared their own shadows, and began to show less initiative in their work.

Take, for instance, Party and Soviet resolutions. They were prepared in a routine manner, often without considering the concrete situation. This went so far that Party workers, even during the smallest sessions, read [prepared] speeches. All this produced the danger of formalizing the Party and Soviet work and of bureaucratizing the whole apparatus.

Stalin's reluctance to consider life's realities, and the fact that he was not aware of the real state of affairs in the provinces, can be illustrated by his direction of agriculture.

All those who interested themselves even a little in the national situation saw the difficult situation in agriculture, but

Stalin never even noted it. Did we tell Stalin about this? Yes, we told him, but he did not support us. Why? Because Stalin never traveled anywhere, did not meet city and kolkhoz workers. He did not know the actual situation in the provinces.

He knew the country and agriculture only from films. And these films dressed up and beautified the existing situation in agriculture. Many films pictured kolkhoz life such that [farmhouse] tables groaned from the weight of turkeys and geese. Evidently, Stalin thought that it was actually so.

Vladimir Ilyich Lenin looked at life differently. He always was close to the people. He used to receive peasant delegates and often spoke at factory gatherings. He used to visit villages and talk with the peasants.

Stalin separated himself from the people and never went anywhere. This lasted ten years. The last time he visited a village was in January, 1928, when he visited Siberia in connection with grain procurements. How then could he have known the situation in the provinces?

Once, [Stalin] was told during a discussion that our situation on the land was a difficult one and that the situation in cattle breeding and meat production was especially bad. [From this] there came a commission charged with the preparation of a resolution called "Measures toward the further development of animal husbandry in kolkhozes and sovkhozes." We worked out this project.

Of course, our proposals at that time did not cover all the possibilities. However we did chart ways in which animal husbandry on kolkhozes and sovkhozes could be boosted. We proposed to raise livestock prices so as to create material incentives for kolkhoz, MTS [machine-tractor station] and sovkhoz workers in developing breeding. But our project was not accepted, In February 1953 it was laid aside entirely.

What is more, while reviewing this project Stalin proposed that the taxes paid by kolkhozes and by kolkhoz workers should be raised by 40 billion rubles. According to him, the peasants were well off and a kolkhoz worker would need to sell only one more chicken to pay his tax in full.

Think about what this implied. Forty billion rubles is a sum which [these workers] did not realize for *all* the products which they sold to the State. In 1952, for instance, kolkhozes and kolkhoz workers received 26,280 million rubles for all products delivered and sold to the State.

Did Stalin's position, then, rest on data of any sort whatever? Of course not. In such cases facts and figures did not interest him. If Stalin said anything, it meant it was so – after all, he was a "genius," and a genius does not need to count, he only needs to look and can immediately tell how it should be. When he expresses his opinion, everyone has to repeat it and to admire his wisdom.

But how much wisdom was contained in the proposal to raise the agricultural tax by 40 billion rubles? None, absolutely none, because the proposal was not based on an actual assessment of the situation but on the fantastic ideas of a person divorced from reality.

We are currently beginning slowly to work our way out of a difficult agricultural situation. The speeches of the delegates to the Twentieth Congress please us all. We are glad that many delegates have delivered speeches [to the effect] that conditions exist for fulfilling the sixth Five-Year Plan for animal husbandry [early]: not in five years, but within two to three years. We are certain that the commitments of the new Five-Year Plan will be accomplished successfully.

(Prolonged applause.)

Comrades! If we sharply criticize today the cult of the individual which was so widespread during Stalin's life, and if we speak about the many negative phenomena generated by this cult (which is so alien to the spirit of Marxism-Leninism), some may ask: How could it be? Stalin headed the Party and the country for 30 years and many victories were gained during his lifetime. Can we deny this? In my opinion, the question can be asked in this manner only by those who are blinded and hopelessly hypnotized by the cult of the individual, only by those who do not understand the essence of the revolution and of the Soviet state, only by those who do not understand, in a Leninist manner, the role of the Party and of the nation in the development of the Soviet society.

[Our] Socialist Revolution was attained by the working class and by the poor peasantry with the partial support of middle-class peasants. It was attained by the people under the leadership of the Bolshevik Party. Lenin's great service consisted of the fact that he created a militant Party of the working class, but he was armed with Marxist understanding of the laws of social development and with the science of proletarian victory in the fight with capitalism, and he steeled this Party in the crucible of the revolutionary struggle of the masses of the people.

During this fight the Party consistently defended the interests of the people and became its experienced leader. [The Party] led the working masses to power, to the creation of the first socialist state. You remember well the wise words of Lenin: that the Soviet state is strong because of the awareness of the masses that history is created by the millions and tens of millions of people.

Our historical victories were attained thanks to the Party's organizational work, to the many provincial organizations, and to the self-sacrificing work of our great nation. These victories are the result of the great drive and activity of the nation and of the Party as a whole. They are not at all the fruit of Stalin's leadership, which is how the situation was pictured during the period of the cult of the individual.

If we are to consider this matter as Marxists and as Leninists, then we have to state unequivocally that the leadership practices which came into being during the last years of Stalin's life became a serious obstacle in the path of Soviet social development. Stalin often failed for months to take up some unusually important problems, concerning the life of the Party and of the State, whose solution could not be postponed. During Stalin's leadership our peaceful relations with other nations were often threatened, because one-man decisions could cause, and often did cause, great complications.

In the past [few] years, [after] we managed to free ourselves of the harmful practice of the cult of the individual and took several proper steps in terms of [both] internal and external policies, everyone [has been able to see] how activity has grown before our very eyes, how the creative activity of the broad working masses has developed, and how favorably all this has acted upon economic and cultural development.

(Applause.)

Some comrades may ask us: Where were the members of the Politbiuro? Why did they not assert themselves against the cult of the individual in time? And why is this being done only now? First of all, we have to consider the fact that the members of the Politbiuro viewed these matters in a different way at different times. Initially, many of them backed Stalin actively because he was one of the strongest Marxists and his logic, his strength and his will greatly influenced [Party] cadres and Party work.

It is known that after Lenin's death, especially during the first years, Stalin actively fought for Leninism against the enemies of Leninist theory and against those who deviated. Beginning with Leninist theory, the Party, with its Central Committee at the head, started on a great scale work on the socialist industrialization of the country, on agricultural collectivization, and on cultural revolution. At that time Stalin gained great popularity, sympathy and support. The Party had to fight those who tried to lead the country away from the correct Leninist path. It had to fight Trotskyites, Zinovievites and rightists, and bourgeois nationalists. This fight was indispensable.

Later, however, Stalin, abusing his power more and more, began to fight eminent Party and Government leaders and to use terroristic methods against honest Soviet people. As we have already shown, Stalin thus handled such eminent Party and State leaders as Kosior, Rudzutak, Eikhe, Postyshev and many others.

Attempts to oppose groundless suspicions and charges resulted in the opponent's falling victim to the repression. This characterized the fall of comrade Postyshev.

In one of his [exchanges] Stalin expressed his dissatisfaction with Postyshev and asked him, "What are you actually?"

Postyshev answered clearly, "I am a Bolshevik, comrade Stalin, a Bolshevik."

At first, this assertion was considered to show [merely] a lack of respect for Stalin. Later it was considered a harmful act. Eventually it resulted in Postyshev's annihilation and castigation as an "enemy of the people."

In the situation which then prevailed, I often talked with Nikolay Alexandrovich Bulganin. Once when we two were traveling in a car, he said, "It has happened sometimes that a man goes to Stalin on his invitation as a friend. And when he sits with Stalin, he does not know where he will be sent next – home or to jail."

It is clear that such conditions put every member of the Politbiuro in a very difficult situation. And, when we also consider the fact that in the last years Central Committee Plenary sessions were not convened and that sessions of the Politbiuro occurred only occasionally, from time to time, then we will understand how difficult it was for any member of the Politbiuro to take a stand against one or another unjust or improper procedure, against serious errors and shortcomings in leadership practices.

As we have already shown, many decisions were taken either by one person or in a roundabout way, without collective discussion. The sad fate of Politbiuro member comrade Voznesensky, who fell victim to Stalin's repressions, is known to all. Characteristically, the decision to remove him from the Politbiuro was never discussed but was reached in a devious fashion. In the same way came the decision regarding Kuznetsov's and Rodionov's removals from their posts.

The importance of the Central Committee's Politbiuro was reduced and its work was disorganized by the creation within the Politbiuro of various commissions – the so-called "quintets," "sextets," "septets" and "nonets" Here is, for instance, a Politbiuro resolution from October 3, 1946:

"Stalin's proposal:

"1.The Politbiuro Commission for Foreign Affairs ('Sextet') is to concern itself in the future, in addition to foreign affairs, also with matters of internal construction and domestic policy.

"2.The Sextet is to add to its roster the Chairman of the State Commission of Economic Planning of the USSR, comrade Voznesensky, and is to be known as a Septet.

"Signed: Secretary of the Central Committee, J. Stalin."

What [sophistry]!

(Laughter in the hall.)

It is clear that the creation within the Politbiuro of this type of commissions – "quintets," "sextets," "septets" and "nonets" – was against the principle of collective leadership. The result of this was that some members of the Politbiuro were in this way kept away from participation in reaching the most important state matters.

One of the oldest members of our Party, Klimenty Yefremovich Voroshilov, found himself in an almost impossible situation. For several years he was actually deprived of the right of participation in Politbiuro sessions. Stalin forbade him to attend Politbiuro sessions and to receive documents. When the Politbiuro was in session and comrade Voroshilov heard about it, he telephoned each time and asked whether he would be allowed to attend. Sometimes Stalin permitted it, but always showed his dissatisfaction.

Because of his extreme suspicion, Stalin toyed also with the absurd and ridiculous suspicion that Voroshilov was an English agent.

(Laughter in the hall.)

It's true – an English agent. A special tap was installed in his home to listen to what was said there.

(Indignation in the hall.)

By unilateral decision, Stalin had also separated one other man from the work of the Politbiuro – Andrey Andreyevich Andreyev. This was one of the most unbridled acts of willfulness.

Let us consider the first Central Committee Plenum after the 19th Party Congress. Stalin, in his talk at the Plenum, characterized Vyacheslav Mikhailovich Molotov and Anastas Ivanovich Mikoyan and suggested that these old workers of our Party were guilty of some baseless charges. We cannot rule out the possibility that had Stalin remained at the helm for another several months, Comrades Molotov and Mikoyan probably would not have delivered any speeches at this [20th] Congress.

Stalin evidently had plans to finish off the older members of the Politbiuro. He often stated that Politbiuro members should be replaced by new ones. His proposal after the 19th Congress to elect 25 persons to the Central Committee Presidium was aimed at the removal of old Politbiuro members and at bringing in less experienced persons so that these would extol him in all sorts of ways.

We can assume that this was also a design for the future

annihilation of the old Politbiuro members and, in this way, a cover for all shameful acts of Stalin, acts which we are now considering.

Comrades! So as not to repeat errors of the past, the Central Committee has declared itself resolutely against the cult of the individual. We consider that Stalin was extolled to excess. However, in the past Stalin undoubtedly performed great services to the Party, to the working class and to the international workers' movement.

This question is complicated by the fact that all this which we have just discussed was done during Stalin's life under his leadership and with his concurrence; here Stalin was convinced that this was necessary for the defense of the interests of the working classes against the plotting of enemies and against the attack of the imperialist camp.

He saw this from the position of the interest of the working class, of the interest of the laboring people, of the interest of the victory of socialism and communism. We cannot say that these were the deeds of a giddy despot. He considered that this should be done in the interest of the Party, of the working masses, in the name of the defense of the revolution's gains. In this lies the whole tragedy!

Comrades! Lenin had often stressed that modesty is an absolutely integral part of a real Bolshevik. Lenin himself was the living personification of the greatest modesty. We cannot say that we have been following this Leninist example in all respects.

It is enough to point out that many towns, factories and industrial enterprises, kolkhozes and sovkhozes, Soviet institutions and cultural institutions have been referred to by us with a title if I may express it so – of private property of the names of these or those Government or Party leaders who were still active and in good health. Many of us participated in the action of assigning our names to various towns, rayons, enterprises and kolkhozes. We must correct this.

(Applause.)

But this should be done calmly and slowly. The Central Committee will discuss this matter and consider it carefully in order to prevent errors and excesses. I can remember how Ukraine learned about Kossior's arrest. Kiev radio used to start its programs thus: "This is Radio Kosior." When one day the programs began without mentioning Kosior, everyone was quite certain that something had happened to him and that he probably had been arrested.

Thus, if today we begin to change the signs everywhere and to rename things, people will think that these comrades in whose honor the given enterprises, kolkhozes or cities are named also met some bad fate and that they have also been arrested.

(Animation in the hall.)

How is the authority and the importance of this or that leader judged? On the basis of how many towns, industrial enterprises and factories, kolkhozes and sovkhozes carry his name. Is it not about time that we eliminate this "private property" and "nationalize" the factories, the industrial enterprises, the kolkhozes and the sovkhozes? (Laughter, applause, voices: "That is right.") This will benefit our cause. After all, the cult of the individual is manifested also in this way.

We should, in all seriousness, consider the question of the cult of the individual. We cannot let this matter get out of the Party, especially not to the press. It is for this reason that we are considering it here at a closed Congress session. We should know the limits; we should not give ammunition to the enemy; we should not wash our dirty linen before their eyes. I think that the delegates to the Congress will understand and assess properly all these proposals.

(Tumultuous applause.)

84

Comrades! We must abolish the cult of the individual decisively, once and for all; we must draw the proper conclusions concerning both ideological-theoretical and practical work. It is necessary for this purpose:

First, in a Bolshevik manner to condemn and to eradicate the cult of the individual as alien to Marxism-Leninism and not consonant with the principles of Party leadership and the norms of Party life, and to fight inexorably all attempts at bringing back this practice in one form or another.

To return to and actually practice in all our ideological work the most important theses of Marxist-Leninist science about the people as the creator of history and as the creator of all material and spiritual good of humanity, about the decisive role of the Marxist Party in the revolutionary fight for the transformation of society, about the victory of communism.

In this connection we will be forced to do much work in order to examine critically from the Marxist-Leninist viewpoint and to correct the widely spread erroneous views connected with the cult of the individual in the spheres of history, philosophy, economy and of other sciences, as well as in literature and the fine arts. It is especially necessary that in the immediate future we compile a serious textbook of the history of our Party which will be edited in accordance with scientific Marxist objectivism, a textbook of the history of Soviet society, a book pertaining to the events of the Civil War and the Great Patriotic War.

Second, to continue systematically and consistently the work done by the Party's Central Committee during the last years, a work characterized by minute observation in all Party organizations, from the bottom to the top, of the Leninist principles of Party leadership, characterized, above all, by the main principle of collective leadership, characterized by the observance of the norms of Party life described in the statutes of our Party, and, finally, characterized by the wide practice of criticism and self-criticism.

Third, to restore completely the Leninist principles of Soviet socialist democracy, expressed in the Constitution of the Soviet Union, to fight willfulness of individuals abusing their power. The evil caused by acts violating revolutionary socialist legality which have accumulated during a long time as a result of the negative influence of the cult of the individual has to be completely corrected.

Comrades! The 20th Congress of the Communist Party of the Soviet Union has manifested with a new strength the unshakable unity of our Party, its cohesiveness around the Central Committee, its resolute will to accomplish the great task of building communism.

(Tumultuous applause.)

And the fact that we present in all their ramifications the basic problems of overcoming the cult of the individual which is alien to Marxism-Leninism, as well as the problem of liquidating its burdensome consequences, is evidence of the great moral and political strength of our Party.

(Prolonged applause.)

We are absolutely certain that our Party, armed with the historical resolutions of the 20th Congress, will lead the Soviet people along the Leninist path to new successes, to new victories.

(Tumultuous, prolonged applause.)

Long live the victorious banner of our Party – Leninism!

(Tumultuous, prolonged applause ending in ovation. All rise.)

www.ingramcontent.com/pod-product-compliance
Lightning Source LLC
Chambersburg PA
CBHW060159290526
45789CB00003B/1081

* 9 7 8 1 4 6 8 1 0 1 0 0 3 *